The Memoir and the Memoirist

THOMAS LARSON

THE MEMOIR AND THE MEMOIRIST

Reading and Writing Personal Narrative

Swallow Press / Ohio University Press • Athens

Swallow Press / Ohio University Press, Athens, Ohio 45701
www.ohio.edu/oupress

Printed in the United States of America

Swallow Press / Ohio University Press books are printed on acid-free paper ∞ ™

15 14 13 12 11 10 09 08 07   5 4 3 2 1

The epigraph quoted from Annie Ernaux, *Simple Passion,* pp. 8–10, is used by permission of the publisher, Seven Stories Press.

Library of Congress Cataloging-in-Publication Data

Larson, Thomas, 1949–
  The memoir and the memoirist : reading and writing personal narrative /
Thomas Larson.
    p. cm.
  ISBN-13: 978-0-8040-1100-6 (hc : alk. paper)
  ISBN-10: 0-8040-1100-1 (hc : alk. paper)
  ISBN-13: 978-0-8040-1101-3 (pbk : alk. paper)
  ISBN-10: 0-8040-1101-X (pbk : alk. paper)
  1. Autobiography—Authorship. I. Title.

CT25.L28 2007
808'.06692—dc22
                                    2007005958

To Suzanna

How strange that all
The terrors, pains, and early miseries,
Regrets, vexations, lassitudes interfused
Within my mind, should e'er have borne a part,
And that a needful part, in making up
The calm existence that is mine when I
Am worthy of myself! Praise to the end!

—William Wordsworth, *The Prelude*

"Oh, 'Tis Me That Is Wounded"

—Scottish fiddle tune

Art would not be important were life not more important.

—James Baldwin

Once I had dressed, made up, done my hair and tidied the house, if I still had some time left, I would be incapable of reading or marking essays. In a way, too, I didn't want my mind to concentrate on anything else but the wait itself, in order not to spoil it. Quite often I would write down on a sheet of paper the date, the time and "he's going to come," along with other sentences, fears—that he might not come, that he might not feel the same desire for me. In the evening I would go back to the sheet of paper, "he came," jotting down the details of that meeting at random. Then, dazed, I would stare at the scrawls on the paper and the two paragraphs written before and after, which one read in succession without a break. In between there had been words and gestures which made everything else seem trivial, including the very writing destined to capture them. An interval of time squeezed in between two car noises—his Renault 25 braking, then driving off again—when I knew that nothing in my life (having children, passing exams, traveling to faraway countries) had ever meant as much to me as lying in bed with that man in the middle of the afternoon.

It would only last for a few hours. I never wore my watch, removing it just before he arrived. He would keep his on and I dreaded the moment when he would glance at it discreetly. When I went into the kitchen to get some ice, I would look up at the clock hanging above the door: "only two more hours," "only one more hour," or "in one hour I'll be here and he'll be gone." Astonished I asked myself: "Where is the present?"

He would dress slowly before leaving. I would watch him button up his shirt, put on his socks, his underpants, his trousers, then turn towards the mirror to fasten his tie. After he had put on his jacket, it would all be over. Now I was only time flowing through myself.

—Annie Ernaux, *Simple Passion*

Contents

Preface

For several years, I have wanted to write an essay on memoir, to immerse myself in my love of the form as writer and reader. My idea was to dwell on the period from now back to the late 1980s, when memoir burst forth sui generis from the castle of autobiography and the wilds of the personal essay. Like any child, memoir had had its issues with its parent, autobiography. In response, the patriarch, steadfast in its tenets and traditions, didn't want much to do with memoir; so the fledgling ran off to find its own path in the world, going a little crazy with experimentation and daring. On its own for twenty years, the memoir still seems unfettered and undefined. Its persistent self-involvement attests to its exploratory zeal. Even its so-called failings are part of its mission. In our time, memoir dwells in a fleeting paradise, and some of us are trying to preserve the woods before the academic bulldozers enter with reference works and subject heads. To examine this expanse, I have found it best to mix criticism, psychology, reflection, essay, historical and cultural contexts—memoir *is* an American form—as well as my experience and that of others who are writing the form in the 2000s. To ground my ideas, I offer close readings of the important elements of sixteen memoirs.

Among the questions: Why is the form so popular? What is it people are seeking by writing memoir? Why is it that when we write of what we remember, the effect on us *now* is so important? Has the form shown a directional purpose in the two decades of its emergence? Based on my reading of more than one hundred contemporary memoirs and the drafts of student writers, I see memoirists focusing on the emotional immediacy of a singular relationship—unresolved feelings for a parent, a child, a sibling, a partner, an illness, a regret, a loss, a death, a phase like childhood or adolescence, a period like college. As they tell their stories, some authors expand the personal to such larger issues as heritage, gender, ethnicity, culture, the spiritual and natural realms, even time itself. In memoir, it doesn't matter whether the primary relationship is long past or recent or even current, as long as the telling is relational and honest.

Self and that which the self contends with in the world make up one nexus. Another is the meeting between a past self and a present self, one or both impelling the writer's insights now. Memoirists engage these selves by using the dramatic techniques of narrative, characterization, and description as well as the analytic styles of explication, essay, and reflection. With such stylistic possibility, much tension is created when self and other, now and then, drama and analysis are joined. The tension hurls us into a kind of vortex, whirling judgment, dizzying memory. The only way out of the vortex is to face the truth or, rather, face the paradox of *telling the truth.* In memoir, we don't just tell the truth. We use the possibilities of the form to guide us into a process by which we try to discover what the truth of our lives may be.

Watching memoirists explore the possibilities of the form, I've been aided by Northrop Frye's *Anatomy of Criticism,* in which he calls literature "an inexhaustible source of new critical discoveries" (6). Memoir is offering to readers and writers its own inexhaustible discoveries, proving itself adept as a literary form and as a means of self-disclosure. I would say that a memoir imaginatively renders our evolving selves and critically evaluates how memory, time, history, culture, and myth are expressed within our individual lives. To understand *how* the memoir has become a new literary form in our time is the reason I've written this book.

Acknowledgments

Gratitude goes to the many who helped steer me toward writing *The Memoir and the Memoirist*. Those from my groups (some of whose words and stories appear in these pages): Kay Sanger, Joan Mangan, Ollie McNamara, Paul Havermale, Sheila Fisher, Tami Dumai, Sue Norberg, Steve Montgomery, Linda Hutchinson, Patrick McMahon, Felicia Castro, Stephen Gallup, Chi Varnado, Allan Rudick, Dolores Forsythe, Julie Meola, Deborah Johnson, Wendy Gelernter, Marcia Aguiniga, Susan Stocker, Anita Trevino, and Kim Harlow (I have changed a few names in the text where necessary). Those who commented on the manuscript or listened to my ideas: John Christianson, Marc Lampe, Nancy Cary, Roger Aplon, and Judy Reeves. My sons, Jeremy Vincent Larson and Blake Ellington Larson, and my brother, Jeff, none of whom asked to have a memoirist in the family and all of whom have been gracious about my proclivity to write about our relationships. I owe thanks to Judith Moore, who died of cancer while I was finishing this book. Judith, the author of a stunning memoir, *Fat Girl: A True Story*, was my editor at the *San Diego Reader*, for which I've written narrative nonfiction the last eight years. Not only did she keep me working constantly on new stories these past eight years, but she also enthusiastically supported what I wrote, both memoir and journalism. She was my William Maxwell, on the phone and via e-mail, and she never knew how much her intelligence and love of good writing influenced me. I wish I had told her. Finally, I appreciate the enthusiasm and skill of the staff at Swallow Press/Ohio University Press: marketing manager Jean Cunningham, project editor John Morris, and director David Sanders.

To my second-half life-partner, Suzanna Neal, I want to say that the greatest gift you've given me is criticism with love. Simply by asking, What are you trying to say? Suzanna showed me where to make the crucial cuts and where to put the emphasis. How much her intelligence and love of good writing have influenced me. Suzanna has been thrilled by my successes and understood my failures as a writer. In those moments I treasure her expression: when she puts her arms around me, raises herself onto her toes, and pulls me close to her out of desire and possession. "At the end of my life," writes Rumi, "with just one breath / left, if you come then, I'll sit up and sing."

This Writing Life Now Is What I've Lived For

An Introduction

It's summer in Southern California, and I'm teaching a nine-week course, Writing the Memoir. Fifteen beginners have assembled, among them Chi, Patrick, Ana, Paul, and Kay; one's a nurse, another's a retired designer of women's clothing, another's with the city. They hail from towns like Ashtabula, Ohio, and Lubbock, Texas, from cities like Brooklyn and Los Angeles. They tend to be older than younger, more curious than careful. The first thing I say, which I've learned from my own memoir writing, is that you must forget about writing an autobiography. After four or five decades, you'll spend another ten years trying to get a whole birth-to-date life on paper. Even if you succeed, it's a good bet that no one, other than your family, will read the eight hundred–page opus. Besides, once Mom or Dad or little brother reads it, they'll want changes, which you probably won't like. What's more, if you attempt to write the whole story, you must paddle back up every tributary of your developmental stream, exploring less the clouded depth of your experiences and more the surface shimmer of years, roles, griefs, and dreams.

You must, I tell them, see the past as dividable. List and reflect on your life's thematic centers. Search for a temporal phase or an emotional thread. Love affair, profession or abiding interest, a single geographic or psychological journey, a lost political belief. Which one has greater weight than the others? To write memoir is to be selective; to write one's autobiography is to be indiscriminate. Another point: the theme or story may be centered in the recent or the long-ago past. (People, like great novels, have themes, though a person's theme can change.) Time and memory may or may not have made the story less raw. Still, you need to emphasize that which captivates you in the present. Don't worry about remembering events: they have already shaped themselves in your mind and emotion, though you should be on guard for how *you* reshape them as you write today.

The class turns to discussion. One man grew up gay in Pocatello, Idaho, and asks, Can that be my story? One woman is the recent recipient of a heart transplant at sixty-two. Is it too soon to write about it? Some question while others listen intently. I sense ease, their comfort growing; they've come to the right place. Already cohesion is building, a like-mindedness. One commonality is that memoir's currency has brought them in. They've read *The Kiss* and *Angela's Ashes, The Liars' Club* and *The Color of Water.* They've treasured the honesty in these authors, felt their compulsion to get down the child-parent drama. They're aware of nobodies whose memoirs have rocketed them to stardom, been celebrated and exploited in the media. New Age mariners, group members aren't afraid to confess; they welcome collective process. Many recognize that their writing will happen only as it's spurred by the group. They sense also that I will lead them. They seem to trust the memoir form to guide them because it is open to all—not exactly a literature of the people, but, certainly, of any individual.

The second week, I repeat ideas about theme. You must comb through a dozen or more themes in your life, each unique, each book-length. Choice requires a stick-to-itiveness, one that resists the memoirist's natural urge to love being lost in the forest of the self. If you can't see the focus yet, take a single event, a relationship, even an image, and explore it for a week or two. In this way, we continue with exercises, readings, discussion. I suggest they write an exploratory eight pages; raw is better than refined. Around week four their first attempts arrive. One isolates a mother's dying farewell, another conjures her trip to Cuba in the 1970s. Each piece is read aloud by the author and critiqued by the class. What are we looking for? I call it the "heat." Where—page, paragraph, or sentence—is the writing alive with a felt intimacy? Where does your attention rivet, your skin go galvanic? Where do you hear the writer affected by what she reads? Where do complaint and nostalgia weasel in, where does the narrator become defensive? One night a woman who has been asking me for more exacting guidelines, which she thinks I've got clasped in my hand and will not share, utters a sudden truth.

"God, this is hard," she says.

"Good," I reply. There's chagrined laughter. *Good.* Your toes should feel the precipice. What's so hard about memoir? I ask. Samples of frustration. Trying to find which part of my life is the best part to unlimber right now. Trying to see that other parts, just as vital, may not pertain to the part I've chosen. Trying to understand why my life has had so many beginnings. Trying to identify which of my past selves still confound me. Trying to discover why I remember things differently than others do, either about me or about shared experience—and why I remember things differently today than I did five years ago.

Fifteen are now twelve, and these hardy ones press on. Soon, they want to examine the controversies of memoir. Primed by nattering editors and critics, the group worries that memoir is tainted and untrustworthy. It's become a lurid, gut-spewing enterprise, whose reputation is suspect because its ubiquity is thought to subsume its artistry. Anybody is an author. The form is regularly slighted as exhibitionistic, confessional, whiny. They've read the headlines in the oft-dismissive *New York Times:* "Woe Is Me. Rewards and Perils of Memoir" or "We All Have a Life. Must We All Write About It?" The group feels sullied by the East Coast elites. They feel seduced and spurned by the publishers, carnival bosses who want acts of murder, sex, and abuse, preferably all three—and little else. In despair, one says, "Who's ever going to want to read about my two years in Costa Rica in the Peace Corps, thirty-five years ago? No one was murdered. No one was raped."

As we go, I get something unexpected. The class is pursuing *me*. They want me to enlarge on the memoirs I've read and studied, the writers I've worked with as an editor, the life-writing I've done, the ways my pieces have affected those I've written about, and the ways my life has changed because I've written about my major relations: father, mother, children. What is washing over them, they insist, must have already washed over—and enlightened—me.

WHAT I KNOW comes from teaching, reviewing, and writing memoir for the last two decades. My pursuit, bolstered by the current cultural push, is born of character: I am fascinated by the art and science of memory, personal literary criticism, and the different forms of autobiography, biography, and memoir. A few years ago my story "California, Here I Come" was published in the *San Diego Reader,* where, as a contributing writer, I specialize in narrative nonfiction. The piece told of how I decided in 1982 that by moving my family (my wife and our young twin sons) to California, I could save our crumbling marriage, an emotional lie which had entrapped us. Not only did the promise of sun-kissed California hasten the marriage's collapse, but the breakup unleashed something unexpected. I had always hated the inauthentic in others, so when I saw how it had taken over my life, I was horrified. I began to see how my self-deceit had buried my once-intact self-identity. That self, which I regarded as artistic and which I had cultivated before the marriage, was long gone, exiled and unconscious. The new person, when told he had to work at a minimum-wage job, put his fist through the wall. That was *me,* whose shame I had to feel concurrently with the failure the divorce brought up before any sense of my core artistic self would return. The tale my long story for the *Reader* tells is about a family's fall as well as my change into a person *less* self-deceitful, what California culture in the 1980s was so good at freeing me to do.

I had torn through the caul; divorce had freed me. Indeed, I had no idea how fully I was locked in a bad marriage, no idea how fully I was the jailer. I don't think it's an overstatement to say that, during the mid-1980s, I got myself through the pain and back to sanity by writing. At first I tried to write the story into a novel. But it felt false, derivative, distant. I longed to discover what I felt (memoir), not invent what I might have felt (fiction). A few years after the breakup, I taught an undergraduate class in modern American literature. I had read James Baldwin's fiction in graduate school when I wrote my thesis about left-wing and minority writers in America. I decided to teach his *Go Tell It on the Mountain* (1953), a novel about a black kid who becomes an adolescent preacher in 1930s Harlem. Intrigued that the novel was based on Baldwin's life, I turned to his essays to learn more. Those autobiographical pieces, particularly the title essay of his 1955 collection, "Notes of a Native Son," were extremely moving. True, Baldwin's invective about racial tension and the power such racism has over those who hate often dominates his thought. But his narrative writing about his family reveals the universal stickiness of our parents' lives: whatever has angered and disillusioned them often rears up as unresolved themes in their children. Whether parents are alive or dead doesn't matter. Their vulnerabilities and paradoxes live on in us.

Baldwin's father's hatred of white people is so intense that it transforms the teenage Baldwin before he has had his own episodes with racist whites (which come soon enough). The son's path is clear: not to let his father's malice poison him but, instead, as he writes in "Notes of a Native Son," "to hold in the mind forever two ideas which seemed to be in opposition": liberating himself from the anger which is also necessary to his fight against injustice. Baldwin says that hate begins "in the heart and it now had been laid to my charge to keep my own heart free of hatred and despair" (84).

Surely, this was an African American sensibility, one historically and community-determined. Baldwin's kith and kin have no doubt benefitted from his personally emancipatory essays and his politically motivated novels. But what came through for me, a white middle-class Midwesterner, was Baldwin's blooded inheritance, which, infected by his father's bile, was his and his alone to repair were he to be free.

At once, I felt an emotional parallel in my life. My father had his own store of hatred—it wasn't racial but religious and class-based. Argumentative by nature, he was a seminary student in the Catholic Church and fought with the priests about God's purpose following the mass deaths of the First World War. He quit seminary and the church and went to college. There, he studied fine arts (he was a talented designer) but, because of the Depression, he left his artistic calling for commerce. Next, the Second World War waylaid him with what he described as three years of boredom on a naval supply ship. After the war, he became a salesman and, eventually, a marketing director for a St. Louis paper company. By the 1960s, however, he was miserable, in large part because he had turned his back on his calling. Another factor: my father struggled his entire life with obesity. Throughout his childhood, my older brother Steve, who was bigger than my father, got the brunt of Dad's wrath. I escaped the onslaught because I was athletic and not fat. In fact, I was shamelessly favored while Steve was cruelly teased. Because I was better and compliant, my father would confide his hatred of work to me, rationalize his despair. His three sons needed feeding, he'd say; Mother's "lifestyle"—a Lincoln Continental, country club fees, carpet cleaning, color TV—needed funding. Feuding with Steve, a fat man's diet, and office politics took their toll. He would have two heart attacks, the second of which, at sixty-one, killed him, a couple months into retirement. That was 1975.

Marriage and a postwar family had set my father on a career track where promotions were keyed to long hours and company servility. The work was soulless, and its tedium was killing him. Plus, because of his complaints, no promotion was forthcoming. When he told me all this, I said he should quit. But he didn't quit. He just ground it out, year after year. Feeling his desperation, I tried to be empathetic. Along with my friends, many of whom had bitter fathers as well, we blamed the business world for our fathers' collapse. We choose paths in the arts or education. Plus, we thought that sensitivity to our fathers' entrapment would keep us from repeating the walling-in of ourselves by career, marriage, and children. Not a chance. Families bring us our fate. My father, like Baldwin's father, had a morbid sense that the American male had no choice but to be enslaved. This feeling that both men shared—though the suffering from racial discrimination was no doubt much greater—lodged in my mind as it had in Baldwin's. Eventually, as a young father, I became overweight and depressed, hated the jobs I had to do to earn a living. My own misery grew and, at times, I lashed out at my wife and at friends. And yet I was fortunate. The hell realm my father had been sentenced to lasted, for me, only a few years. As painful as that summer I got divorced and became homeless was, my father's wound was finally laid bare.

The moment I woke up to the father-son pattern, it cowered and weakened.

Later, after my older brother Steve died in 1989—a heart-attack victim at forty-two, he had inherited our family's heart disease—I began writing about, that is, remembering and refeeling and grieving, the strain between my father, my older brother, and me. Soon I was including my mother, a younger brother, sons, an ex-wife, lovers. How did these diverse people relate emotionally and psychologically to me and to each other? How did this affect my sense of self? Sorting all this out became my occupation.

I discovered that I had come to defend the doltish low-wage work I did as necessary, much as my father had. I had taken little responsibility for nurturing my artistic talent, cursing others instead. It was easy to justify my failure to pursue my artistic dream by identifying with my father. As I wrote about my phases, I read memoir, those fearless authors like Frank Conroy and Geoffrey Wolff who had endured some version of what my family had endured. These writers revealed the monolithic nature of our prisons, be they social, intellectual, familial. I learned that anyone who could narrate his condition and its development within his family could be freed from that condition. The way out of the cell—and the means to stay out—came for me through writing memoir. The tales I read about real families and the tales I told about mine took me beyond self-discovery. Memoir writing and writing about memoir enacted in my life a purpose for my life. Fifteen years into this process, I have found that memoir has led me to two of my deepest sensibilities: the psychology of adult development and the art of critical discovery.

The trouble is, these sensibilities, as potent as they are, are also buried the deepest. To stay connected, I must try to be honest about myself and those, like my father, I write about—above all, try to be honest about the slipperiness of telling the truth. I say *try* because honesty is never simple. And telling the truth, to ourselves and to others, guarantees emotional anguish. In fact, trying to be honest about the difficulty of unearthing what's painful may be the truest thing one can do. I'm not alone in feeling this way. Hundreds of thousands of people, not just writers, rely on devotional and therapeutic practices by which they can inquire into the truth of their lives. Memoir is one practice, and it has ascended for this generation because the form is so useful in getting at the truth. To be useful, of course, aggravates postmodern thinking. But I have found that memoir's pragmatism is its genius, limiting neither the possibility of the form nor the expression of the author.

AT THE GROUP'S last class, several read their latest excerpts, critique one another with an authority that's also tempered by regret. One woman declares, "How will I ever know why you left your husband?" Suddenly it's 9:30. I offer praise, thanks, wish them luck. Into the night we go, each to our locked cars, I leave last, intending to move on, where, I'm not sure, though I'm unconcerned.

Outside the door, eight are huddling, buzzing quietly.

"Good night—" I say.

"Wait!" says one, who startles me.

"We don't want this to end," says another. "Is there any way we can keep meeting? We just got started." She's a bit upset. "You can't abandon us."

Another woman asks whether I would consider continuing. "We'll pay you to lead us," she says. "We'll meet at one of our homes." Ollie, our seventy-three-year-old matriarch, volunteers her living room. "You won't have to do any preparation. Just facilitate."

How curious. And yet it shouldn't be, given the power of the group and the form, which I discover are lashed together. As to their request, I'm grateful: I don't want to lose them either. But I'm also uncertain, fearing a dependency. And yet their élan is irrepressible. What I don't want to lose—I see this now—is their memoir-in-the-making, what they are undergoing and I get to witness. I want to stay close to them as adults, in whom writing memoir is a living entity, the mature transformations of an unfinished person and an unfinished life. And though it takes time, those self-transformations, as the writer works through them, will complete themselves as stories. These people I am getting to know as memoirists I will know as memoirs. How can I let go of *that?*

WEEKS LATER, a group of eight begins meeting twice a month. One reads, the rest comment. I speak last, hoping to help each writer balance, where possible, self-exploration and her self-selected theme. One guideline I return to is that whatever we've witnessed, we've also participated in. And the act of writing memoir allows us to continue participating in what we've witnessed. Writing memoir means that we combine what happened with how the exploration of what happened continues to affect us. After forty-six years, Julie is writing a memoir. Part of her turbulent past has flooded in, and, she thinks, her life now is one of remembering. Her focus on a long-gone phase has her believing that the past is the seat of her emotion, more so than the present. The past drama, however, is not the only drama. The present drama of recollection is equally alive, equally *in* and *of* the story. Julie is finding that as she remembers she is being emotionally altered by what she remembers. She is discovering things she never knew she knew. And it is this startling alteration of herself—to be drawn in deeper, to be surprised by what she didn't know or half-remembered, to be enthralled about her choices and her fate more than she has ever been—that galvanizes her writing. What Julie is learning is that as a memoirist This Writing Life Now is what she has lived for.

1

From Autobiography to Memoir

Autobiography and the Autobiographical Essay

For the last century and a half, the world of life-writing, which includes biography, autobiography, memoir, and confession, has been dominated by the personal tale of a public figure, a life socially significant in his or her own time. Autobiographies issue from such luminaries as Ulysses S. Grant, Helen Keller, Malcolm X, and Bill Clinton. The great-person-turned-writer thinks of his life as a series of causative events: childhood begets adolescence, adolescence begets youth, and so on. The author thus organizes the work in strict chronology, usually dabbing in enough of the parents' past to bring about his birth. (Readers will recognize a format similar to biographies.) As the life collects its periods and phases, the tone becomes self-justifying and is often trained on moral experience. The author's purpose is to set the historical record straight, an idea based on the assumption that there is a single record and that the person who lived it can best document it. A good writer might tell a gripping story, but it's not a requirement. What is required is that the author must have accomplished something notable—he may be a scientist whose discovery eradicated a disease, or a military leader whose campaigns were decisive—in order that the tale be written.

Despite the occasional female author, autobiography is a male genre. Such books typically promulgate career, heritage, social standing, or fame. In England and America, tall tales of the great man include *The Education of Henry Adams* (1907), in which Adams charts his development as an intellectual in the third person, and T. E. Lawrence's *The Seven Pillars of Wisdom* (1926), which is the self-mythologizing reminiscences of his fighting alongside the Arabs who revolted against the Turks in 1916. Books written by public figures have at times been labeled "memoirs," a literary genre, also concerned with historical events. Rendering the public life means leaving the private life either underdeveloped or ignored. What remains is commonly a tabulation (though it may be exciting to read) of whom one knew and what one witnessed— seldom what one felt. Autobiography and one's "memoirs" generally avoid introspection and scenic drama and, instead, summarize the significant people and events in the author's life.

In *The Norton Book of American Autobiography,* Jay Parini tells us that autobiography "might well be called the essential American genre" (11). This would be accurate were the form widely practiced. But it hasn't been. In fact, its exclusivity as the story of a notorious or exceptional figure has probably censored more formal life-writing than it has encouraged. Parini, I think, wishes that autobiography were America's genre because he's enamored of a few very good books, two in particular: Franklin's *Autobiography* and Henry David Thoreau's *Walden*. Like armies massed at Gettysburg, these works pit two autochthonous New World lives against each other: Franklin's book tells of how his thrift found a home in the burgeoning American economy, while Thoreau's tells of how his thrift opposed that economy's intrusions into the place-sustaining lives of Americans. In both stories, the authors attest to their liberation, often more ideologically than experientially. The tales represent political visions, endemic to this country, quite well. In Franklin's conservative vision, the idea of liberation is harnessed to sin, going against the moral authority of God or church: whatever you're freeing yourself from means you've already overdesired it. In Thoreau's liberal view, the idea of liberation is harnessed to freedom from narrow-mindedness or enslavement; indeed, some can only be free when they are politicized and seize their rights. (With the *Narrative of the Life of Frederick Douglass, an American Slave* [1845], a work that predates Thoreau's, the title tells us that his tale is a personal testament to and a call for the release of a bound people, slaves and former slaves like Douglass. Yes, he's the one who's freed, but he portrays his freedom as an example to others.)

Leonard Kriegel has noted of Franklin's *Autobiography* that "there is something missing . . . something essential, an absence not merely of the deeper self but of the very possibility of a deeper self" (213). I read America differently than Parini does: the deeper self *is* essential to American writers and artists but is not found in traditional autobiography. Unless you lived a life as consequential as Douglass's or Franklin's, you wouldn't have (in the last two centuries) been drawn to write your life story, let alone think of it as such. Without a publisher's blessing, your biography would not have been written, either. About the closest you would have come to anything full-length and life-assessing might have been the confession, a religious work in which your failings as a sinner would have been assuaged by your atonement. Indeed, some older confessionals are remarkably *inner,* albeit ideologically beset, in their focus. And yet despite the conditions that severely limited who actually wrote an autobiography, American writers have written *autobiographically.* Which is to say, they have used personal experience in story, essay, poem, or travel account—in the short form—in service of a larger subject.

The autobiographical essay has, especially in the twentieth century, flourished as an alternative to, even a comment on, the overwrought life story. As a memoir-essay, personal narrative, or personal essay, by either known or unknown authors, this compact piece has been published in newspapers, magazines, and literary journals. (The personal essay's most important innovator was the Romantic era's William Hazlitt. As Phillip Lopate has written, Hazlitt "brought a new intimacy" to the form, "establishing as never before a conversational rapport, a dialogue with the reader" [180].) One of the greatest essayists, who uses the direct personal style in much of his work, is George Orwell. His 1931 tale "A Hanging" ranks among the finest short memoirs ever written. The piece tells of a Hindu man who, during the British occupation of Burma, is hanged in "classy European style," that is, dispassionately and efficiently. The piece shudders with the Orwellian notion of a blithe state torturing a debased individual as it also glows with a familiar participatory truth. The idea that a personal narrative could be as exciting and intimate as a Hemingway tale has taken time to sink in, in part because the form has had to play second fiddle to the narrative invention of fiction. It wasn't until Orwell's several examples ("Shooting an Elephant," "Marrakech," and "How the Poor Die") and those of writers as diverse as E. B. White and Zora Neale Hurston had captured readers with their participatory narrators that the form gained currency. (Of course, today, short and long sections of personal narrative grace books on psychology, economics, travel, science, even literary criticism, by authors whose direct experience gives their subjects greater weight.) The short memoir piece is spare, universal, confessional, and true. Who among us has not been touched by what is perhaps the best personal essay by an American, Joan Didion's "On Self-Respect," first published in *Vogue* in 1961?[1]

The Memoir

It may be that the memoir has risen in the last two decades because the personal essay expanded its singular theme and fleshed out its emotional immediacy. It may be that the life story shrank its garrulous, self-important voice. In either event, the hull of traditional autobiography began to leak sometime during the 1980s. It was then that a new kind of storytelling emerged: short and midlength books, sometimes called memoir, in which the author *chose* a particular life experience to focus on. Heralding the new in particular were three books of intense interior drive: Vivian Gornick's *Fierce Attachments: A Memoir* (1987), a story of mother-daughter closeness in which both, disturbingly, inhabit each other's pasts; Tobias Wolff's *This Boy's Life: A Memoir* (1988), a tale in a boy's voice of his peripatetic mother and cruel stepfather that reads like a novel with fiction's narrative punch; and Richard Rhodes's *A Hole in the World: An American Boyhood* (1990), a harrowing story of two brothers who endure the abuse of a tyrannical mother and the neglect of a hapless father. Such books felt new, in part, because they lacked the scope of autobiography and the limitation of the essay.

Another publishing event, in 1995, also reshaped our sense of what memoir might be. This was the publication of the unexpurgated edition of *The Diary of a Young Girl* by Anne Frank.[2] The new edition included material Anne's father, Otto, excised from the original when he first published her diary in 1947: Anne's insight into his character, her budding and more explicit sexual feelings for Peter, and the anxiety she had about herself. Her anxiety was spurred mostly by difficulties she had had with her mother, which she discussed in passages that were also kept out. As great a book as the original edition was, we had not read, for a half century, Anne's most trying revelations about her family, truths which, read now, only deepen her story. The new Anne Frank blossoms as a memoirist: we can finally see *her* as clearly as she once saw those suffering around her.

The emotional concentrations of Gornick, Wolff, and Rhodes, as well as the ever-affecting Anne Frank, all carry that personable voice: diary-like, reflective, intimately close and trusting, at times uncomfortably so. An instance of the latter is Lucy Grealy's *Autobiography of a Face* (1994). Despite the title's playfulness, Grealy details how her interior self was changed by an operation for cancer that surgically took away one-third of her jaw when she was nine. "This singularity of meaning—I *was* my face, I *was* ugliness—though sometimes unbearable, also offered a possible point of escape. It became the launching pad from which to lift off, the one immediately recognizable place to point to when asked what was wrong with my life. Everything led to it, everything receded from it" (7). Engagement with "this singularity of meaning" is emblematic of a new approach to personal narration. As my writing teachers trumpeted, a good topic is a narrowed topic. One emotional or thematic focus is plenty for a book. Indeed, only those parts of Grealy's life that were germane to the shadow and substance of her disfigurement got in.

How simple this is! For two decades, writers have gravitated to this simplicity, whether they were writing about buying a house in Mexico, living with AIDS, or losing a child. Memoir situates the one story as equal to or greater than—even against—the epic chronology of the Life. Autobiography's central tenet—wisdom gained through many years—is much too grandiose for the memoirist. In fact, memoir writers are so bent on activating the particular in their books that many are writing of the immediate past, even the still-corruptible present, not waiting for time to ripen or change what they know.

As the memoir has evolved, the canvas and the frame have gotten a lot smaller. And, to see the new form properly, we have to look more closely and the canvas has to contain more detail—

detail that is revealing and reflective, textured and telling, exclusive and sharp. For example, note how this memoir's subtitle announces its severe singularity: *Heat: An Amateur's Adventures as Kitchen Slave, Line Cook, Pasta-Maker, and Apprentice to a Dante-Quoting Butcher in Tuscany,* by Bill Buford (2006). Buford, of course, is writing autobiographically. But he's hardly writing an autobiography. He's writing memoir. He's focused not on a life but on a portion thereof, a portion small enough to allow him the nitty-gritty he and his readers crave. It's true that critics have conflated autobiography and memoir throughout our literary history. But what we need to do is to sharpen their growing distinction: the memoir is supplanting its uncle, in part by telescoping the form, in part by accruing stylistic innovation. In the last ten years, writers have been distinguishing the form faster than we can analyze their attempts.

Once authors pared down the autobiography and it was no longer recognizable as such, the new form needed a name. It was christened "memoir," and the designation has often been attached as or in a subtitle: *Fried Butter: A Food Memoir.* Twenty years later, the form is recognizable on its own. In the memoir, writers use a modicum of summary and great swaths of narrative, scenic and historical, to sustain their single theme or emotional arc. Thus, Lauren Slater's *Prozac Diary* (1998) concentrates only on a ten-year period which has just ended, when the drug has removed her debilitating depression and she isn't crazy anymore. As the story grows, she discloses to herself, often in surprising ways, the truth about her years of suffering. Slater is guided as much by these revelations as by her memory. She seems to have trusted that in the wake of her disease she could be the most honest with herself, and this honesty would best express the disease. One key is courage: she went at the topic immediately, not waiting for the autobiographer's prerogatives, age and wisdom.

For such emotionally intense memoirs we need emotionally revealing memoirists, authors who are willing to put themselves on the couch, under the lamp, into the darkness, sometimes as they are living or soon after they have lived the emotional mire they are working with and, perhaps, waking up in. The *Encyclopedia Britannica* describes the old plural form, "memoirs," as that which emphasizes "what is remembered rather than who is remembering." If we invert this, we can call a book that emphasizes the *who* over the *what*—the shown over the summed, the found over the known, the recent over the historical, the emotional over the reasoned—a memoir.

Memoir and Memoirist

A word or two about this relationship. Both memoir and memoirist draw attention to the writer now—product and producer. Still, there's something tentative, not quite out of the womb, about the pair. The *ist* in memoirist doesn't have the bona fides that novelist and scientist do. The job description needs codifying: memoir practitioners have no field yet (memoirship) for which, like psychologists, they can hang a shingle. (The field of books analyzing autobiography and memoir as a form is small but growing.[3]) A memoir sounds like a dalliance; there's something purely personal and time-bound about it, like a fall fashion or passing clouds. With autobiography, we think there is only one life—the person lives it, then writes it. Boom, done. But the memoir feels prey to (or is it desirous of?) immediate emotional memory, almost as if the point is to preserve the evanescent.

There's a practical reason for memoir's provisionary status. Once we locate its engine and the emotion with which to make it go, we will find that far more of our lives will be left out than can ever be put in. Leaving so much out adds to the mystery of selection. The memoirist has to limit the project severely, be a master trimmer. Most of us find that through writing memoir we behold the great vistas of our lives, even among our circumscribed phases. We quickly discover, however, that no matter how telescoped our thematic and emotional emphasis is, the story is still *a* story: it is subjective and distinct, a melody with the barest orchestration. It cannot be *the* record of *the* past as autobiography tries to be. Memoir is *a* record, a chamber-sized scoring of one part of the past. Despite its rightness, it's a version of, perhaps a variation on, what happened. We don't really read Jeannette Walls's "childhood" of poverty and neglect in *The Glass Castle: A Memoir* (2005); we read her version of it—which, because it's so well written, we think *is* her childhood. And yet it's something else, too: one path down a set of precisely chosen days of desperation she took in this one book.

Imagine ten siblings, born at one-year intervals, each of whom, on his or her thirtieth birthday, writes a memoir about growing up. Reading those ten memoirs, we would find agreement, in general, only on the barest facts. Everything else—pecking-order differences, stronger and weaker egos, parental favoritism—would be subject to individual perspective, in part because each kid had fought hard to be heard or had wilted in the competition. Which book is true? All are true and none is truer, though each of the ten writers would defend his or her truth forever. Who can say what that family's story is? I've never heard of a single-family bevy of memoirs. Rather, there's usually only one author in the clan. He or she is situationally selected as the most observant one in the group—I'm afraid that's been my lot—who, though she is crowned, can never really be the family spokesperson. Susanna Kaysen's *Girl, Interrupted* (1993) may seem like the story of what happened to her because of her family. But, in the absence of competing views that might refute or refashion or deepen the tale of how she was interrupted at eighteen and why, her memoir is only *her* truth—only her *adolescent* truth, only her *late* adolescent *emotional* truth, only her late adolescent emotional *breakdown* truth—and no one else's, a conclusion I'd wager her parents (who seem selectively absent in the book) would have easily agreed with.

The memoirist, then, is one who while and after she writes realizes the existential limitation of memoir. Private, mythic score-settling, at times given to ax-grinding or ax-wielding terror—and yet true to one rigid but gossamer particularity. I hope the challenge to traditional autobiography and its absolutist view of the self is met. But the construction of a relative self in the memoir is no less difficult: the person writing now is inseparable from the person the writer is remembering then. The goal is to disclose what the author is discovering about these persons. But such a goal can arise only in the writing of the memoir, a discovery which then becomes the story.

2

Discovering a New Literary Form

Who Writes?

Passionate, contrary, innovative, undefined: memoir today has the energy of a literary movement, recalling past artistic revolutions that initiated new ways of seeing. The form has cleared most of the first hurdles, among them the rap that memoir must be tied to family dysfunction. Memoir's diverse topics and authors of all ages squash that prejudice. Indeed, we may be living in the age of memoir. How might we know? Sheer numbers. If you follow Amazon.com's list of the one hundred best-selling "biographies and memoirs," you'll find that on average fewer than 20 percent are biographies or autobiographies (maybe two are religious confessions). The rest are memoirs, by the hundreds, by the thousands. Many of these come from no-name authors who are turning to the form as a means of examining their most intimate relationships. I think of such moving works as Le Anne Schreiber's *Light Years* (1996), a book that juxtaposes her withdrawal from a big-city newspaper and move to a small town with a meditation about the mortality of her father; of William Loizeaux's *Anna: A Daughter's Life* (1993), a tale of a child who didn't reach her first birthday, though her parents and a team of doctors did everything they could to save her. These and hundreds of other emotionally venturesome memoirs share this individuality: Here is what it was like to be *me,* to face what I faced, to lose what I lost.

What is faced and lost is crucial. Only by lingering on something outside the self, with which he has had intimate experience, can the author disclose himself. Memoir is a relational form. Loizeaux does not just describe *his* torment as his daughter died of a host of congenital difficulties. He deals with the effect on his marriage, the doctors and hospital staffs with whom he and his wife became close, and the personality of Anna herself, who had four months at home with her parents before she succumbed. On the surface, the book is about her life and death. But, more importantly, it is a book that allows her life and death to bring out the emotions and changes that her father endured. Anna's living and dying brought about a book in which Loizeaux could remember and mourn his daughter, *be* the person who lost her. As Khalil Gibran has said of the parent's possessiveness toward his children, "they come through you but not from you." It is remembering this child's coming through Loizeaux that becomes the memoir.

Immersing himself in Anna's passage, Loizeaux finds that it is bigger than any passage in the chronology of his life. Since he does not treat her life within the autobiographical overview of his, he can examine and linger on the multiple layers of its particular hell. (The autobiographer seldom has time to layer any phase; this is the main structural difference between it and the memoir.) A story with a limited temporal scope encompasses not less but more material. The author might explore his hopes and delusions; the cracks in his persona; his culture's attitude toward loss before and after a death; his insecurity with how he remembers what did and didn't happen; how trauma reconfigures his extended family—any of which may be germane to his telling. Linking experience to one's persona, one's culture, one's ideas, the memoirist uses dramatic narrative and reflective analysis to bridge the details and the expanse of what he's unleashed. Story alone won't do it. The memoir's prime stylistic distinction is a give-and-take between narration and analysis, one that directs the memoirist to both show and tell.

Let's say you plan to write a memoir about the year you just spent rebuilding homes in New Orleans, post-Katrina. What's relational? Beyond musing about the stultifying bureaucracy and the force of a natural disaster, you decide to focus on the displaced people you saw every day who want their homes fixed and their city back. You detail their initiative and frustration, their loss and vulnerability. But what of *you* is important in all this? Is it your homelessness—actual, emotional, symbolic—that has been stirred by their trauma? Put another way, perhaps helping others has led you to reflect on the meaning of displacement, or alienation, in your life, too. It must have something to do with your core self or else you wouldn't have volunteered, you wouldn't have felt *your* passion connected to theirs. Self and world, self and core; all this is relational.

In memoir, how we have lived with ourselves teeter-totters with how we have lived with others—not only people, but cultures, ideas, politics, religions, history, and more. This balancing act of the self in relation to the outer and the inner worlds, against the memoir's thematic and temporal restrictions, fascinates me. What is it that makes a person become who she is, perhaps has always been? What is it that changes us? How much of the self is innate, how much of it learned? What role does self-delusion play in our identities? What is it that makes us seek the mythic entitlements of American life differently from our neighbors? Most Americans think that the better among us are self-driven like Franklin or self-actualized like Thoreau. Such idolatry props up the great-man fiction, the "I did it my way" myth, a stepwise deterministic view of life that autobiography has engendered and memoir is challenging.

And yet the "I" of the memoir can also be the subject of the work. How do I understand the person I was then in light of the person I am now? This *I-then* and *I-now* (the pairing comes from Virginia Woolf) rings in memoir's paradox. Though much time and many realizations may separate these two I's, it is nigh impossible to keep the voices of today's narrator and of yesterday's narrator apart. They are always in flux, an example of which I will describe shortly. The thinking goes, *my* story is also *his* story; the person I am, I was—or I was, I am. Here I am in high school, in 1967, and yet that person is not me now. He is another. Still, don't I share his traits, whether or not they are readily expressed? The truth is two-sided: I am not exactly him nor am I free of him. It feels natural to see the remembered self as a character who has an independent life, chooses for himself, indulges free will. But memoirists avoid such self-casting. The memoir writer does not situate himself in a recreated world as though he were a literary character. What the memoirist does is connect the past self to— and *within*—the present writer as the means of getting at the truth of his identity.

Before writing *The Liars' Club,* Mary Karr thought she should fictionalize herself: "When I tried to write about my life in a novel, I discovered that I behaved better in fiction than I did in real life. The truth is that I found it easier to lie in a novel, and what I wanted most of all was to tell the truth" (Karr, cited in "The Family Sideshow"). Truth is uppermost in the minds of memoir writers because veracity won't let them be. So as not to embarrass the living, they may rename people and places; they usually re-create dialogue since there's no word-for-word record; and they may dramatize an event that differs from the recollections of others who were there. Sometimes memoirists must make life-and-death choices. Azar Nafisi, still fighting the Muslim theocracy in Iran, prefaces her *Reading Lolita in Tehran* (2003) by stating that "I have made every effort to protect friends and students, baptizing them with new names and disguising them perhaps even from themselves, changing and interchanging facets of their lives so that their secrets are safe."

But, even in a post–James Frey world, memoir writers are not fashioning fictionalized autobiographies or autobiographical novels, as one or two critics contend. Most memoirists do *not* falsify their pasts so as to build a better story.[1] The best honestly explore how they recall the past and what of themselves is and isn't true. Before I go a step further, I want to be clear about memoir and fiction, a confluence I'll return to often. Memoir is related to fiction because memoir, like fiction, is a narrative art: we narrate past events; always, as we write, memory tells us stories. We must guard against our own narrative gullibility. We must ask ourselves, Did it happen as I remember? Have I misremembered and, if so, how will I know? We may have *some* means at our disposal to verify the past: letters, journals, family records, others' recollections. But we must understand that often our memories have erased and altered things before we search out their latest version or a version from someone else. The nature of memory, as any brain doctor will confirm, is to mix imagination and fact. But that is not the same as saying that as memoirists we can riddle our tales with fictional composites and Hollywood endings. Still, in the memoir, the truth and figuring out the truth abide. The best way to deal with the tension between fact and memory, as one uncovers the tension in the course of one's writing, is to admit to the tension—not to cover it up.

One reason for this confusion between memoir and fiction, between how memoir and autobiography overlap, is that the memoir form, so newly emerged, is less understood than written. Function noses out form: writers write, and analyze what they've done only *after* they've written. It's this avidity to leap in and get at one's past and present selves that's so contagious among authors, both first-timers and pros. The hoped-for reward is self-knowledge, not self-mystification. The writing will guide us there, if we write and reflect on what we write. But, though my pep talk may sound empowering for the author, the writing alone can lead to despair. Many give up: trying to make sense now of then incurs sudden, resistless anguish. The material may get too hot to handle.

Joan, the woman in my writing group with the transplanted heart, desperately wants to tell that story—how she was a candidate on the waiting list for two years, six months of which were spent in the hospital; how two transplants failed, the first "harvest" (she was given twelve minutes to get to the hospital) canceled once bruises were discovered on the donor's heart and the second called off by an ice storm in Oregon that delayed the plane's arrival; how the third try was successful and she joined a family's loss of their son, whose sudden death must be a part of her tale. One scene she'd like to write: waking to the shock of having a man's heart in her chest and hers *gone,* and then wondering how long his will keep beating. But she can't write that scene. Not yet. Joan's vitality is easily sapped (she says she has one-third the energy of the normal person), and then there's her mother's illness to deal with every morning before she gets to her desk.

The quotidian gives Joan plenty to work with, but now another fin cuts the surface. Before her surgery, Joan was locked in with no past or future—she could only wait, in dread and hope, for another's death. A few years later, when she begins writing (a friend took notes during her surgery and recuperation), she is overcome by grief. A man has died and she has lived: two unrelated beings are now inextricable. What is she remembering? Is it the shock his heart suffered from the loss of his body? Is it the trauma of her twice-thwarted expectation that two harvests came to naught? Is it the responsibility that she must live for both? Now these and other emotions well up in eerie, invasive detail until she has to stop: The writing she attempts goes only so close to the experience, then won't go any closer. Everything she is writing now she is discovering now, and every discovery now *must be felt*. The heart-fullness allows her to live. But there is much strain, ebbing from the conflicted hearts of her memory, and to tell it all may be impossible.

Now and Then: Virginia Woolf

The first personal narrative to interweave the author's I-now and I-then is Virginia Woolf's stunning and incomplete "A Sketch of the Past." This ninety-five-page memoir-essay was posthumously published with four other pieces under the title *Moments of Being*. (The history of its publication is interesting: "A Sketch" was first published in 1976; its second half, reworked and expanded by Woolf, was discovered in 1980, necessitating a second edition in 1985 of the "complete" "Sketch.") The work is diary and journal, meditation and memoir, written sporadically during 1939 and 1940 and planned as her autobiography. It may be only coincidence that these were difficult years for Woolf because of the threat of war, which she engages forcefully in the piece. Woolf went no further than what amounts to a second draft. She died, a suicide, in March 1941, four and a half months after the final entry in the "Sketch." A series of a dozen dated entries, the book is fragmented, undisciplined, and impassioned: Woolf, at age sixty, mainly recalls her mother, father, sisters, brothers, half sisters, and half brothers and her family's summer home at St. Ives in Cornwall. Her most disturbing admission is that her stepbrother Gerald Duckworth fondled her "privates" when she was thirteen. As in her novels, Woolf details individual lives and places with animated and felt imagery. She microscopically enlarges her most precious memories. To our joy, she is incapable of giving equal weight to equal events. She ends the time of her recollections around 1900, when she was eighteen. A world gone forty years ago. And yet not gone at all.

The beginning ten pages are a salvo in which Woolf reflects on how her memory will shape this very remembrance she is writing. Her perceptions are briefly examined, then exampled in the remaining pages. At the onset of the second entry, she discovers "a possible form for these notes." She would like to remember the past by making "the two people, *I now, I then,* come out in contrast" (italics added). She believes the past is or should be "much affected by the present moment," though her remunerative task at hand is to finish the biography of art critic and Bloomsbury friend Roger Fry. Thus, she "has no energy at the moment to spend upon the horrid labour that it needs to make an orderly and expressed work of art" (75).

The self-consciousness of the opening pages is beguiling. The book Woolf didn't write, and the one she left us, may be better than any we might imagine. (In part, Woolf is known for the thoughtful development of ideas and emotions in her intimate diaries, letters, and essays. Though less artistically composed than her novels, her personal writing abounds with inspired commentary.) The first entry of "A Sketch" is written at Monks House, near Rodmell, Sussex, and the River Ouse, on Tuesday, April 18, 1939. Before her family memories (some going back more than fifty years) become the focus, Woolf considers how she remembers, what memory means, what "one's memoirs" might be. All of a sudden, consideration turns to criticism and she begins thinking about new methods of representing the self and the past. She first says that most memoirs are failures because the writers "leave out the person to whom things happened" (65). They err on the side of overnarrating events, and gossip, instead of uncovering the character of the rememberer, a character alive as much now as then. To flesh out the author, it is important to know who the parents were, their class, their proclivities. It is more crucial, however, to know the *perception of the rememberer*. Woolf follows suit, recalling first pictures—a nursery and the sensual feelings of St. Ives's air, beach scenes, wave sounds. So strong are these memories that she tests them against a view of her present surroundings. "At times," she writes, "I can go back to St. Ives more completely than I can this morning. I can reach a state where I seem to be watching things happen as if I were there. That is, I suppose, that my memory supplies what I had forgotten, so that it seems as if it were happening independently though I am really making it happen" (67).

How marvelous that she reports her mental state in the throes of remembering early childhood. She does not merely catalog the past, nor tell the psychiatrist the lurid details. Her own psychotherapist, she moves from analysis to objective fact to a self-possessed intimacy. She is aware of her present "rapture" with recollecting St. Ives. And then, as quickly as she raises the ship of the past, she questions its seaworthiness. She writes that life makes childhood memories "less strong . . . less isolated, less complete" by adding "much that makes [memories] more complex" (67). Looking back over an accumulation of years gives memories their depth. More is made of them as we mature; we need to cherish or resolve what is recalled. The question is, can such memories ever be recollected for what they were? Woolf says no. To revisit such brief scenes and moods is "misleading, because the things one does not remember are as important; perhaps they are more important" (69). The more important the memory, the harder it is to retrieve. But memories are imprinted and, because of their imprint, contain wholeness. Woolf labels such memories "exceptional," which means the few and the intense. For her the exceptional memory always possesses "being," while other parts of life—conversation, meals, weather, train rides, running a press, waiting around (Woolf says the unconsciousness of life is "a kind of nondescript cotton wool")—comprise "non-being" or boredom (70–71).

The exceptional moments are "moments of being" (70). They are physically overwhelming and, over time, represent a legendary quality about the self. The moments require days and weeks of unexceptional life to pad and pace the distance between them as moments. The quotidian life is a complement to these peaks of being. Moments are enlarged by our memory; this grandiosity makes much about the past seem more exceptional than it probably was. Moments are self-selective: they highlight, expand, overpower, and change the past. Moments argue for their being as they wrangle with the present to be heard, to be part of a dialogue, to frame the picture of, at least, a part of one's life. Woolf becomes animated by this idea. Given the time and the calm, the ideal way to write her life would be to contrast the intense present, one being-full and intense, with a part of the past, itself equally being-full and intense, and make their dueling exceptionalities work on each other.

Without doubt, the present is full of being: England is under attack. What would the past recollected during this dire present be like were she to write of it under these imposed conditions? Woolf ventures forth. Her first attempt is placid, before the bombing of London has begun, while the second is much different because it includes the bombs.

On July 19, 1939, Woolf has just returned from an uneventful crossing of the Channel. Before she writes about one of her stepsister Stella Duckworth's lovers, she longs to recall the past because the present is running "so smoothly." It is like the "sliding surface of a deep river." "Then one sees through the surface to the depths. In those moments I find one of my greatest satisfactions, not that I am thinking of the past; but it is then that I am living most fully in the present. For the present when backed by the past is a thousand times deeper than the present when it presses so close that you can feel nothing else" (98). How curious that a smooth present is tantamount to seeing the past smoothed of its turmoil.

But once the bombs start falling on London, everything changes. The destruction agitates Woolf about how and what she remembers. Upset, she recalls the pain of so much unexpressed feeling for her parents. She begins "venting that old grievance" once again. Her mother died prematurely and her father, whom she "alternately loved and hated," became a ward to his daughters, particularly Stella and Vanessa. That sullied thought shifts her back to the present. Aflutter, she enquires of her husband Leonard whether he thinks there's a "third voice" between the past and the present that can express her "vague idea." She wonders "whether I make up or tell the truth when I see myself taking the breath of these voices in my sails and tacking this way and that through daily life as I yield to them." She wonders if anyone cares: "Which of the people watching the incendiary bomb extinguished on the hill last night would understand what I mean if they read this?" (133). Remembering her difficult aging father and a Nazi bomb in her midst isolates her in rough seas. To calm down, she recalls sailing at St. Ives, which momentarily stabilizes the lurching. To calm down, she tries taking control of the present so she can take control of the past.

Is Woolf suggesting that what we remember about ourselves can be—perhaps should be—influenced or changed by present circumstances? Is she suggesting that depending upon the degree of unsettlement, the past can mislead the present as much as the present misleads the past? If the past's moments of being are what we tend to recall, while the present mixes, pell-mell, being and non-being, must we write out of an exceptional present whose energy, in turn, ignites a more luminous portrayal of the past? Does it matter that who we are can change who we were? Won't the past always be the same in memory, whether we are rushing to a bomb shelter or disembarking from an uneventful passage over the English Channel?

Such are the questions Woolf posed about her life and, by extension, our lives as well. I think of Woolf's "Sketch" as the gauntlet to this generation of memoir writers. On one hand, this probing memoir is enthralling because it's unfinished. Woolf may have left off completing this autobiography because she was forced to deal with the raw emotions the work unleashed in her life. Attempting a memoir about a past that felt sketchy and disruptive during the daily scare of an expanding war may have brought a sense of failure on her, which her depression only worsened. Memoir, too, can usher in a tragic consequence. Recalling life's disappointments may lead a writer back to a past where the exceptional moments are all bad ones, which, in turn, rain doom (like German bombs) upon the present. On the other hand, Woolf's incompleteness, her mulling over the possibility of the form itself as she *writes* the form, is just as enthralling. She gives birth to a radical idea—the interconnectedness of past and present in the act of memoir writing—which is as profound and lasting as anything else she bequeathed us in her work.

3

The Past Is Never Over

The Remembered Self and the Remembering Self

What many memoirists of the past twenty years have discovered—
some following Woolf's lead—is how much the *intervention* of
the rememberer, the person writing now, is pertinent to the work.
Intervention may sound heavy-handed. But I mean it as the degree to which memoir writers are attentive to the interplay of the
story and their remembering the story, and how this interplay
helps an author discover herself. I realize there should be a concise
definition for the memoir—a book about an important or difficult relationship or phase in the author's life. But such a subject-
or theme-focused definition begs the question: What actually happens as we write and remember that becomes the memoir's narrative? Recall Mary Karr: "What I wanted most of all was to tell the
truth." But what is this truth? Where does it exist? In memory? In
the writing? In the intermixing of the two? Anyone who wants to
tell the truth soon learns that the truth may not want to be told.

It may like staying holed up in its lair, bouldering exit and entrance. Truth-telling requires a kind of demystification of the ever-mystifying notion of how memory works. To get at the truth (fact and emotion) of what happened, we must understand, as concretely as we can, what the past is and how we relate to it in the present.

Barrett J. Mandel analyzes the shell-game quality of memory, its tendency to be, like electrons, moving and fixed simultaneously. Mandel says that memory is paradoxical. On the one hand, he writes, "I can trace events with my memory, I can peruse old documents, study snapshots, and speak to others who affirm that my past actually occurred." On the other hand, "I have to admit that it often seems as if my past, or at least my memory of it, has *not* remained fixed." Mandel cites an example: one day he finds out that one of his "cherished elementary school memories never occurred—or not in the way I had always remembered it." The event he recalled was a "screen memory . . . a vivid and totally convincing substitution of a less painful version of reality than one which a person is willing to accept as his or hers. My past, I learned, wasn't fixed at all. As vividly remembered as it was . . . I had to relinquish it for another past—the one which has now been labeled the real one. In short, 'my' past changed" (76–77).

What we learn in memoir writing is that memory has far more of its own agency than we thought, that the very act of remembering may alter what did occur. This altering, Mandel says, is key. "Since my past only truly exists in the present and since my present is always in motion, my past itself changes too—*actually changes*—while the illusion created is that it stays fixed" (77). If the past is both fixed and unfixed, then it is always in process. And, not surprisingly, this process lies in the present where our minds and feelings make sense of the past as we recollect the past. Mandel calls this active participation with memory "presentification." He stresses that memory cannot exist without a present stage on which to unfold: "This presentification is not a distortion of any so-called *real past;* this *is the only way 'my life' comes to me"* (83; italics in original).

Mandel's estimation of memory as a present act has great import for the memoirist. The memoir writer works now, writing and remembering. Woolf's remembrances of a difficult childhood were wedded to her current fears of war. Those fears drove her to recall the past in a way that would have been different had the bombs not been falling and the family tragedies not been mounting up. Thus, our present situation means everything to how and what we remember. From this we can extrapolate several relationships that are anchored in present-time remembering. For one, as Mandel suggests, what we remember may or may not be accurate. It has been altered and may be altered again by our recollecting. For another, our remembering selves can rouse us to action today. The past may impinge on the present, but the present can also direct the past with a purpose. What comes back in memory may no longer dominate our lives; however, the recollection may require us to re-evaluate it. My mother's miserly affection, which I experienced as a boy and attend to in memory today, can debilitate me now just as it did then. And I can also take responsibility for that feeling and deal with it, not let it run or ruin my life.

Let's say I'm writing about my first year in college, for me a traumatic year: I dropped out because of a failed love affair. Writing about it, I find three levels operating: first, the events of that year that I can establish via letters, photos, a journal, and others' reminiscences; second, the events of that year that I've recalled (no doubt revised and re-evaluated) numerous times in the intervening years; and third, the event of my writing about it today pushing me to say why that year and the end of the romance remain important. Thus, the drama of that first year in college appears to me the writer as an event in its time, as an event processed in the times in which it's been recalled from then to now, and as an event I'm dealing with today.

This layered simultaneity, time over time, is the prime relational dynamic between the memoir and the memoirist: the remembering self and the remembered self.

In *Lost in Place* (1995), Mark Salzman tells of his teenage devotion to kung fu and his fall from its embrace. In one passage, Mark's father tells his son that some of his bravado from the martial arts that he's learning is, well, ridiculous, and that Mark, even at fourteen, should be questioning what his teacher is telling him. His father punctuates his mini-lecture by saying, "Just be yourself, Mark. You'll do just fine as you are" (60). In response, Salzman writes a paragraph in which he argues with his father and with himself about the meaning of this phrase. He does so by abutting his remembered (1975) self and the intervening selves (roughly 1975–94) who have thought about it. First is his reaction to his father, what he, Mark, was feeling *at the time,* and second is his mature, later-in-life reaction to what his father was posing to him, what he has felt *over time.*

> Be yourself! What a can of worms he opened there. Of course I was trying to be myself! That was the whole point of the kung fu; to become the me I thought I ought to become, instead of some half-assed loser. Anyway, who was to say who I really was? I didn't even know *that*—that was half my problem right there. All I knew was that when you're a really little kid, your parents praise you when you do something they like. If you do something they don't like, they say, "You're not the sort of person who does that! Don't try to be somebody you're not! Be yourself!" So maybe, I reasoned, being yourself means being the person your parents or teachers want you to be. Do we have anything to do with who we are at all? As we get older, we

think of ourselves as having unique personalities, and we take credit for these personalities when we do something good, as if we created these personalities ourselves. But maybe we didn't! Maybe our personalities were shaped by how people around us responded to us. So who are we? As I said, this was a can of worms I didn't care to dip into—at least not that day. (60–61)

We can hear the voice of the narrator shifting from the defensive feeling of the moment to the more "reasoned" feeling that comes with writing and with time. *This is how I felt that day and this is how I have also felt about how I felt since that day.* Thus, Salzman isn't content merely to dramatize the scene with his father, staying "in character," that is, in the fourteen-year-old's self-consciousness. He intercedes from *now:* with explanatory narrative he shows us that he understands what he's writing about—it is still a source of conflict that the writing is helping him work through—namely, the difficult truth about growing up, getting "used to disappointment" (68). Accepting disappointment is Salzman's theme, the thing that defines his father's life and that Mark must come to know about himself and their relationship. While this theme is embodied in the story, it is the memoirist's current examination and editing of his younger self that propels the book beyond a chronicle of adolescence to a memoir of self-disclosure. Simply put, Salzman's voice, in this passage and in many others, is honest about what he's discovering he did and didn't know and, thus, one we trust.

Salzman juxtaposes remembered and remembering selves with flawless ease. Many of us miss seeing the mix as *craft* because the author keeps the story moving. Only at set moments does Salzman intercede in this manner; instead, he keeps the narrative drama strong and the self-changing chronology (the rise and fall of kung fu and other adolescent interests, which eventually disappoint him) central. But the psychological impact of the narrator's self-knowledge in memoir (knowing what when) is also central. It's the memoir's primary compositional conflict: voices from then to now are constantly revising what we remember. Those voices, collected over time and spoken now, may best reflect how we perceive ourselves, having lived with ourselves as long as we have.

The Present Overtakes

Mark Salzman's mixing of narrative voices in *Lost in Place* is the result of much revision, of his listening to and adding in those voices as he drafted. It is also the result of time passing, first as he discovered the "disappointment" story and second as he filtered it through his memory and his sensibility. Enough time lets our many-voiced narrators speak, listen, and interact. This is one reason why writers come to the memoir: they feel that a sufficient amount of passing time will clarify their present perspective. But what of a memoir writer who has not yet lived past the time of her story, who is shaken as it unfolds in her current life and yet is drawn to write of it anyway?

One woman who has been trying to uncover her story is Sheila, a member of my memoir-writing group. Her struggle to find the person she is writing about is always apparent. She begins by focusing on her first marriage. As a senior in high school, she dates a man, Jerry, who's two years older. They go steady, break up, get back together, and eventually marry. She recalls getting married as what she was supposed to do, being "naive on my part." With no children, Sheila spends much time making a structured home for Jerry, with dinner on the table at 5:30 sharp. But Sheila suspects something is wrong. Jerry has become quieter, complaining that he's not sleeping well. He has terrible dreams and is frustrated with his small business, supplying materials to contractors. One of his problems is with work. He refuses to work for anyone else, fearful of having his reading disability discovered. (Sheila says this was not identified at the time but was probably dyslexia.) She doesn't know to what extent Jerry's business is failing because he will go weeks without speaking to her. Sheila has a dreadful feeling that he's in psychological danger. She can feel his foundering in depression. She begins to wonder, in her writing, *when and how* she knew this. One night Jerry doesn't come home; she calls his business but there's no answer. She calls the police and reports that he's gone missing. The next day, she calls the police around noon. They tell her they cannot file a missing person's report for several days. This is a Tuesday. By Wednesday, with no word from Jerry or the police, Sheila drives to the business with a friend. They climb a fence, smell exhaust fumes coming from a closed-up warehouse, and find his parked car. Jerry's rigged a hose from the tailpipe into the car window. He's killed himself.

It's a stunning and disturbing story, and the group and I are curious where this opening volley will take her. And then we hear the second installment. Eight months after Jerry's suicide, a man named Martin calls her, someone she once dated in high school. He has heard she is widowed and asks to see her. He is interested in psychology and in her plight; Sheila, who is open and vulnerable, responds favorably to him the next two years. Amateur shrink Martin begins taking Sheila apart. While they date, she is under a psychiatrist's care. She tells me, in an e-mail, that those sessions consisted of "his asking me a question and my answering with uncontrolled sobbing. We did not get very far." Feeling that she must choose between her psychiatrist and her psychologist, Martin, she chooses the latter and marries him. Once they move to San Diego, Martin becomes "more verbally abusive than ever. He had always been analyzing me, my motives, my life, and continually making me feel bad about myself." It's not long before Sheila seeks treatment from another psychiatrist, who ends up helping her divorce Martin. At the time, she writes, "I realized I had married two different men [Jerry and Martin] with major psychological problems, and I vowed not to remarry until I felt I would not attract a person like that." Martin, though, remains a part of her life via frequent phone calls. Seventeen years later, after Sheila has married a third time, she learns one day that Martin, like Jerry, has committed suicide.

For Sheila, the thematic muck is obvious: "I wanted my memoir to be about my long struggle to free myself from attracting suicidal types." Though she knows today that these men died because of their own problems with depression, that fact doesn't settle what's roiled her for decades. She wants to know what it was "about me, without my knowing it, that contributed to their deaths."

Though Sheila's story may sound desperate, she is not herself desperate. At sixty, she is well adjusted; her marriage is good, and she values writing and therapy. The therapy of memoir, however, reopens old wounds, as becomes very clear to her and to us when, a few weeks later, she brings in a third installment. She has written what has just occurred, part of it torn from the week's headlines. One of her friends, a man named Bill who had battled with a woman for years about custody of their fourteen-year-old son, Evan, and had been given a court order to stay away from both the boy and the woman, has killed the boy and himself. After Bill murders Evan and before he kills himself, he calls several friends. Sheila is one of them. She doesn't get the call, but he leaves a message on her machine. He speaks not only of the horror he has just committed but also in a voice that sounds to Sheila like the despairing voices of her first and second husbands were they to have left her messages before suiciding.

In shock, Sheila is grieving the loss of a friend and his son. In writing about her grief, she is unsure what she's feeling. Suddenly, this one event has fused her life and her writing. In the wake of the murder-suicide, Sheila loses the safety in which she was examining how suicide and intimacy cohabit, somewhat safely, in memory. Her life, in its uncanny ability to stay on theme, has got in memoir's way, and it stops her from writing for a while. And yet she tells us that she can't escape the feeling that the deaths of all these men she's known have something in common. What is it? That the world is more out of control *and* more directed than she thought? If true, what is that saying about *her*? She doesn't know. Maybe she's not supposed to.

Sheila's story is unusual in that the very theme of her work—men's suicides—has merged the past with the present. For me, her story dramatically exemplifies the interaction of life and memoir writing. For Sheila, her memoir is now overrun by the changeable present, which, I remind her, is always exercising its dominion over the past. Time has assuaged her theme and time has again blown it apart. Her tale depicts how psychologically alive the body of memory is: it is both an elder, offering the wisdom of experience, and a child, wanting our attention *now*.

After Bill's and Evan's deaths, and, in part, because of the writing, Sheila is thrown into a "debilitating funk." With a therapist, she finds that she has been able to work through the "post-traumatic stress." She wants to begin writing again, and I wonder how Sheila might tell her story.

One way is to tell the tale only from the perspective of the young woman who endured and survived her first husband's suicide. Okay, but how does she limit the emotional participation of the later suicides, which are surely part of how she might portray that younger self? Telling about each suicide chronologically might show a culmination. But each suicide and her feelings may get mixed up. The force of their accumulation is inescapable. These male death-events have already coded themselves as part of her DNA's memory: the code retains a record of its evolution— where it's been, how it's been modified, how it's been expressed. Moreover, today the code is selecting for her emotional survival, insisting that there is no other way to write *this* story than to intermix the years.

If we know that we grow and change as individuals, why do we believe that our memories of traumatic events don't also grow and change? Why do we think that such events are isolated in their time and somehow just as isolated when we recollect them? I want to answer these queries because it seems that we are finally learning that memories evolve as their rememberers evolve. It may be the rightness of this idea that has so many people reaching to the memoir form, perhaps to verify it for themselves as well as to express the potency, both aesthetic and experiential, of remembrance.

Detaching Now from Then

Here is an example of how one memoirist has bridged from the person who is struggling with the past today and the person who struggled *in* the past. Sylvia Fraser's *My Father's House: A Memoir of Incest and Healing* (1987) uses the interplay between now and then to stage and reveal her childhood sexual abuse. Fraser narrates the story of her past abuse in present tense. She discloses in past tense that which she understands today about the past. It may sound disorienting but it's not, for we soon discover why she adopted this form. Writing the book over a three-year period, Fraser brought the past back so vividly into her life that for her emotional security the past needed to be separated from the present. An instance of Fraser's method comes from the second chapter, "The Other." It begins with an account of her current knowledge about her father in the past tense:

> When the conflict caused by my sexual relationship with my father became too acute to bear, I created a secret accomplice for my daddy by splitting my personality in two.

Thus, somewhere around the age of seven, I acquired another self with memories and experiences separate from mine, whose existence was unknown to me. My loss of memory was retroactive. I did not remember my daddy ever having touched me sexually. I did not remember my daddy ever seeing me naked. In the future, whenever my daddy approached me sexually I turned into my other self, and afterwards I did not remember anything that had happened.

Even now, I don't know the full truth of that other little girl I created to do the things I was too frightened, too ashamed, too repelled to do, [sic] the things my father made me do, the things I did to please him but which paid off with a precocious and dangerous power. She loved my father, freeing me to hate him. She became his guilty own partner and my mother's jealous rival, allowing me to lead a more normal life. She knew everything about me. I knew nothing about her, yet some connection always remained. (15)

As the memory heats up and challenges the author to flesh out her feelings, her "other self"—the little girl about to be abused—arrives in present tense. Fraser shifts from her narrator now to the persona, the four-year-old, who was the target of the father's daily sexual advances. Italics highlight the current recovered material, which, as she gets closer and closer to it, becomes dissociated from her adult narrator and is rendered in third person.

Through the bathroom door I hear my father splashing in the tub. Holding my breath, I slide under his bed, grabbing for Smoky [her cat]. Now the bath plug is being pulled. With a gurgle, the scummy water sucks down the drain.

> By the time daddy stomps out of the bathroom, saronged
> in a towel, my other self is curled on his feather pillow, suck-
> ing her thumb and wearing Smoky's dirty pink ribbon. A
> breeze blows the curtains inward, just like the hair of a fairy-
> tale princess, giving her goose bumps. Whose little girl are
> you? (27)

Fraser's "other self" is "sucking her thumb," sprouting "goose bumps" from the inward-blowing curtains. "I" has become "she." And because of the transformation, she achieves something remarkable. The author has merged "I" and "she" in order to juxtapose childhood abuse and adult remembrance. These voices become mutually supportive; working together, they enact the story and the means by which the story can be told. Neither the abuse nor its recollection dominate. They are coequals, as if to say Fraser's true self is a never-ending release from and return to what her child self was forced to endure.

Margaret Atwood noted in a blurb that *My Father's House* reads like "a detective novel—except that the detective is a part of the narrator's self, and so is the murder victim." As the author recollects the events, detective and victim slowly become aware of each other. Fraser's interweaving of these two takes time, and she is careful to prepare us at each juncture. Eventually our recognition of their watery coexistence in her is what intrigues us the most. What's more, these parallel selves call forth the memoir's guiding narrator, who lives now. She sees how complex the multi-timed and many-voiced narrative self can be. She builds a structure to reveal the past in the present tense and in the present intensity of recovered memory. She has the courage to bring the memory back full force, feel it again, then keep it corralled, the horses wildly running at the fence, for the rest of her life.

4

The Voice of Childhood

No Escape from Chronology

Sylvia Fraser builds a book-length structure by intercutting selected times and voices. Indeed, she forgoes narrating a sequence
of childhood events because nothing is as memorable as the emotional ebb and flow around her father's abuse. Tracking the temporal is less important than juxtaposing now and then. Why? The
latter is a true rendering of Fraser's experience of writing and remembering the past from today: as she awakens to the abuse, she
finds that the past continues to live in her now and demands to
be confronted now. And yet, despite the many memoirists who are
erecting cross-temporal frames different from the episodic frames
of autobiography, the work of Fraser and Woolf and Salzman re-
minds us that no memoirist can escape chronology. Be it abuse,
death, grief, a fall off a horse or the rise to the presidency, a memoir is, as tale and as discovery, always *consequential,* even if one
tries narratively to evade or delay the consequence.

Joan Didion's *The Year of Magical Thinking* (2005) is a book written just after her husband, John Gregory Dunne, has died— he was alive one moment, dead the next. It's purposely written in that wake, in the throes of grief and mourning: Didion seeks the self-deceptive elements of loss that are too often and unhelpfully identified as emotional strains one must work through to return to "normal." Didion returns to *no* normal, resolves little, and upsets the idea that grief is a passage or a "stage" that, at least in the first year, she must get through. Instead, she does her best to slow the bad year down, *way* down. Still, she follows a chronology: the day of her husband's heart attack at dinner, her later memory of the events that prefigured it, her writing the book some ten months after his death, once she gets the autopsy report that reveals facts about his final moments she wishes she could recall but can't. Didion intrudes into the story with so much self-doubt and so many questions that, despite the progression of the unfolding year, there's no closure. That's the story: orderly time and the authority of medical reports resolve nothing. There is only the tension of her starting and stopping the narrative, of her hoping to find answers and never finding them.

Chronology in memoir is best examined in tales of childhood or adolescence. In literature such portraits are the bildungsroman, the prescriptive tale of a hero's or an artist's apprenticeship or education. This coming-of-age story is also favored by memoirists. The story of how I grew arises because the adult, the survivor, is ready to tell it. She's also ready because her memory has given her tale wholeness: frames of era, place, generation. We grow from innocence to experience, and, when written, such pieces may reflect what's finished, what's learned. Because we have processed the past thoroughly in our minds and in our writing, the phase appears over. The sports failures, the dating horrors can't get us. And because they're long over, our youthful follies require the least of our adult reevaluations. In addition, the coming-of-age memoir is favored because its ending signals the onset of the adult writer's career—my early life has prepared me to write my tale. Such narratives are often treasures: *Stop-Time* (1967) by Frank Conroy, *Growing Up* (1982) by Russell Baker, *Half a Life* (1996) by Jill Ciment, *Running with Scissors* (2002) by Augusten Burroughs, for example, all chart the clumsiness and self-obsessions of adolescence, which, by the end, feel mythic. As craft, memoirs about youth—at times penned by novelists who may have also written the autobiographical story first as a novel—are long on story and scene and short on summary and reflection.

An autobiography of childhood and adolescence that uses explanatory narrative is Jill Ker Conway's *The Road from Coorain* (1989), whose title gives it away: this Aussie's childhood is spent in the often solitary duties of sheepherding, though her deepest desire is for intellectual fields elsewhere. Conway selects those character-building traits that spur her growth, which will culminate in her becoming president of Smith College, a fact that is unmentioned in the story but is revealed in a note on the back of the book. Still, destiny permeates the book: we read her outback life and her classics-based education, which, taken together, ensure her maturity. In such castle-high chapters as "Childhood" and "Schooling," we see how the feminist is child to the woman.

And yet things don't necessarily get better in books about childhood. Consider that illness typically brings more pain, as John Gunther's *Death Be Not Proud: A Memoir* (1949) shows. Here Johnny's struggle is resisted by the parents for fifteen agonizing months as the boy rallies against a fickly growing brain tumor. How high the moon of a father's hopes, which then crash once the tumor spreads uncontrollably. This seems to be one of the purposes in writing about a childhood, be it tragic, long remembered, or recently endured: to bring order and resolution to its bodily drama. (I say "bodily" because the body is the site of our first memory and also to distinguish such a memoir's emphasis on the body from the mental and spiritual confessions of the latter-year memoir.) The key word here is "drama," and few would argue that in our time no better dramatic story of childhood exists than Frank McCourt's *Angela's Ashes: A Memoir* (1996). The tale was written by a sixty-four-year-old man whose wretched youth ended long ago and yet for whom the child he was—in his hunger, in his Catholic neurosis, in his tenderness toward and hatred of his father, and in the simplicity and strength of his voice—seems every bit alive today.

Still, for all that, it is the rarest of memoirs, a book perfectly tuned to the unadulterated speech of its child narrator. It is a memoir in which the memoirist, the adult-writing-today, seldom, if at all, intrudes. For the role of the memoirist in its creation, we must look outside the book at what McCourt himself has said about the years it took him to become Frankie.

Frank and Frankie

Angela's Ashes is McCourt's tale of growing up in a family ground down by poverty and alcoholism, first in New York City and then in Limerick, Ireland. The misery those twin evils of booze and want bring to his family is the story. And since the story is so emotionally taut, there's no need for the author to draw attention to himself as the rememberer. As written, McCourt's voice embodies the child. He has said that the child's experiences arose from—and are synonymous with—that voice, which recites the grim play-by-play without flinching. *To hear* the voice of the child, in its purity and heart, is to trust the tale and the teller. No doubt the witnessing nature of that voice resonates with every Irish alcoholic family or, for that matter, any alcoholic family.

The book opens in past tense, wanders until it settles into present tense, and rarely returns to past tense. The present tense animates the story's quotidian feel. The opening summary introduces us to McCourt's family: his siblings, his parents' and grandparents' backgrounds, the family's return to Ireland. But once the present-tense storytelling kicks in, it's all shown via scene. The first scene is on the third page. McCourt's father is coming home after a night of drinking: "He's in great form altogether and he thinks he'll play a while with little Patrick, one year old. Lovely little fella. Loves his daddy. Laughs when Daddy throws him up in the air. Upsy daisy, little Paddy" (13). And so on. We are lodged in the moment, and such moments that McCourt recreates for mother, father, grandparents, and siblings become the book.

Soon things turn ugly; the worsening woe of his young life is relentless. Nothing makes Frankie's life easy. Only his and his brother's postadolescent escape to America, in the end, suggests betterment. But even though McCourt details and lingers on his being unheard in the family, the integrity of the book through the monotone of its narration is so strong that I can't help but wonder where the creator who has sentenced his childhood to such a cell is hiding. According to McCourt's testimony—see "Learning to Chill Out," from the indispensable *Inventing the Truth: The Art and Craft of Memoir*—he wrote the memoir twice, in two successive times. First, during much of his adult life, he worked on the book in contrasting vocal and tonal versions (once comic, another time adult "looking back"); and second, he wrote it in one year after he found the book's voice (the *cadence* of the child he was). His essay is not a writer telling us how in the writing he shaped the voice to sound like the person who is speaking/living the action. Rather, the essay chronicles the journey it took to become that voice, to learn for himself the ineffectuality of his many attempts before he discovered how to tell it true. McCourt's prior and analytic self was uncooperative, belligerent, until one day he asked the most self-evident question of all: "Why didn't I just tell my story naturally?" (Zinsser, 77).

Growing up, McCourt recalls, he was "never encouraged to look at [him]self as a future memoirist, never encouraged to look inward." In school, "We were never encouraged to write about ourselves, or about our families, or anything like that. We always had to write about an event in Irish history" (67). He was never "analytical" about his father's alcoholism, the "central event" of his life (66). He admits that when he came to America at nineteen (the closing scene of *Angela's Ashes*), "somewhere in the dim regions of my mind I knew that I felt cheated" (70) by his Irish upbringing, his poor education, his undeveloped inwardness. But, despite the glimmers of consciousness, he was, even in America, stifled by his past. He didn't think he could get into college, he didn't think he could ever be a teacher—both of which he did accomplish, though, to his surprise, it took ten years until he felt comfortable teaching. He didn't think he could give up the Irish mask behind which he had lived much of his adult life. He tried to write the story of his childhood after he retired from teaching at age fifty-seven, in 1987. He failed. Then he tried to find the story as he and his brother, Malachy, performed a theater act based on their childhood experiences. That, too, he writes, "wasn't honest" (77).

And then, "in August of 1994," he tells us, "I started writing *Angela's Ashes*. I was sixty-four years old." "Suddenly—it's on page nineteen of the book—I wrote a sentence in the present tense. 'I'm in a playground on Classon Avenue in Brooklyn with my brother Malachy. He's two, I'm three. We're on the seesaw.' I meant it just as a note to myself for the next day: how to continue. But the next day I continued where I had left off, in the present tense, in the voice of the child on the seesaw. It felt very comfortable, and I just kept going with it." Once he had the voice, he had the story. "It wasn't a linear process," McCourt continues, "though in general the narrative follows the 'Once upon a time' format right to the end. The book was all done in one draft, in one year, with very little rewriting" (78). He also says that close observation of his two-year-old granddaughter "helped me to recover my own childhood, at least subconsciously. I'm not what you'd call a conscious craftsman. A lot of the book was instinct and a lot of it was retrieving my feelings from the past" (79).

It sounds like a self-portrait of a primitive-intuitive, the sort of subject Gauguin wanted to live among and paint. But beware the coloring. A besieged, marred Irish Catholic, McCourt the memoir writer was *not* intuitive. By his own admission, his tale-telling confidence had to be learned: first, through his high school students' curiosity about his father and about McCourt's working-class upbringing in Ireland (McCourt regaled them with stories: *Hey teach, you should write that down!* [his third volume of memoir is *Teacher Man*]); and second, through the dogged "failure" of drafting. McCourt was more stubborn than intuitive. His insistence that he was "never encouraged" reveals how close he is to the wounded child. His comments reveal just how slow and hardheaded he was as a learner, becoming an author via willpower alone. Though he tells us he read widely and thrilled his pupils with tales of Irish misery, that "natural" voice, written on the page, was censored in him—by his background, by the culture of the Irish in America, and by himself. It is all very confounding to hear that the man who was given the seraphic voice of the child is also the man who, in retirement, exhausted from a string of botched attempts to write the memoir (in his sixties, it was *then* or never), stumbled upon the brogue one day at sixty-four. That gift speaks to deliverance and luck and the Christian message of redemption through suffering.

Once the voice is deemed "natural," everything is accounted for—the book's comfort, its booming sales, its readers' affection. As if "natural" were not only a commodity but, like fat, stored for later consumption. A terribly inexact word, "natural" suggests that for years McCourt's voice was lying in wait, inviolable, still aching to be heard. And because it was lying in wait, it had *lasted,* like a true love from college who remains faithful, though only in our minds.

Here I get a bit antsy. If McCourt's "natural" voice had been hidden or unavailable all those years, then its lacuna was not a literary but a psychological problem that bedeviled him: as he says, self-knowledge ("I'm not *what you'd call* a conscious craftsman" [italics added]) is not inborn. There's a kind of authoritarian proposition about the "natural" voice that arises whenever the adult claims—on behalf of the inner child—that "this child who is speaking is the true child and I've captured his nature by using his voice." What we call "natural" is that which we don't want to be responsible for: Oliver Stone's "natural born killers" who are incorrigible, or Muddy Waters' "natural born lover's man," a sex-afflicted male whose impulses can't be reigned in.

What is "natural" is also buried under the collective weight of postmodern literary culture. Postmodernism seems adult, skewed to the ironic and the detached, while the child's perspective seems free and authentic. Why is it that the child's voice is thought to be truer than the adult's? (I can hear readers saying the child's voice is different, not better. Clearly, for McCourt, it was different *and* better, after all his starts and stops.) I don't deny that McCourt enacts the terrors and loneliness that he felt as a boy under his father's thumb. I quarrel with the idea that the voice of the child who feels much and understands little is adjudged the most appropriate for the narrative of how we come of age. I quarrel with the idea that feeling trumps intelligence—it leads to a dead end in the writing and reading and analyzing of memoir. To say that access to one's voice (as a teen, a new father, a Marine, a nun) and the feelings behind it means one has found the way to write a memoir—as McCourt claimed for himself—is limited and misguided. This is not to say McCourt, in all his Rousseauian naturalness, has misguided us. But it is to say that there's something overbeguiling about this voice, something staged, something literary and, therefore, expedient.

For me *Angela's Ashes* is a triumph of artifice, told through a near-perfect storytelling persona, that holds back the willfulness and complexity of the adult's voice. And yet what McCourt says he himself found in the child's telling of the tale is paradoxical: the purer its voice, the more the hand of the purist shaping that voice is seen. Thus, I don't think McCourt has written a "natural" memoir at all. He has written an artful one. We know this, if we stop and think, because hardly anyone writes like McCourt or, for that matter, James Frey in another highly charged memoir drama, *A Million Little Pieces* (2003). Thousands, instead, write like Mitch Albom in *Tuesdays with Morrie: An Old Man, a Young Man, and Life's Greatest Lesson* (1997), whose reflective adult voice is direct and easily followed (two hundred fifty-seven weeks on the paperback best-seller list!). Albom places his impressions of Morrie's dying, from the recent past, side by side with a number of other narrative voices: scene, commentary, topic-oriented chapters that hew to the chronology of Morrie's demise, dialogue between Morrie and Mitch, self-implication (it is *his* story as much as it is Morrie's), Khalil Gibran–like prose slices in italics—all those strands contrasting and coloring one another, in and out of time. An essay-like search for answers emerges to fuel the narrative, which is very different from the pure voice that fuels McCourt's story. I would call Albom's a writerly sounding memoir, McCourt's, a fictional- or literary-sounding one. The latter's tale springs from literature's fount, owing its strength to fiction, not to memoir.

McCourt's book is the autobiography of a voice, writ large. It memorializes childhood by the author's imperative to feel his way through it—as he says, "retrieving my feelings from the past." It renders *a* childhood, the one the exasperated McCourt finally presents to you and me *as* his childhood. But, as I say, it is far less universal than it appears: while I admire what McCourt has done, no one I know, have taught, or have read has attempted anything like it. (The classic naturalistic style Jeannette Walls uses in *The Glass Castle,* which avoids any overt statement or shaping from a present-day narrator, is an exception.) Writers like Sylvia Fraser or Richard Hoffman in *Half the House: A Memoir* (1995) have, in their stories of sexual abuse, depicted their innocent years with McCourt-like voices. But they've also structured their tales narratively and analytically so as to sow and tend the larger fields of time and memory, healing and self-discovery. McCourt isn't interested in self-discovery per se. He's interested in a self purified of its later years, of its longing for childhood. Most contemporary memoir is not so pure. And contemporary memoir is most contemporary when it tries things different from what McCourt has accomplished.

McCourt's style is popular but unrepresentative of the memoir's development and range in our time. True, publishers may lust after such action-filled memoirs. But they don't always get what they want. To read the work of Blake Morrison, Elizabeth Fox Gordon, Larry Woiwode, and others is to see how narrative and reflection interbreed and conflict in birthing that which is wholly new. The time-traveling narrator, as the British literary critic David Leon Higdon writes in a different context about time and literature, is "both a recorder and an investigator, whose act of looking back changes him" (101). That is the payoff. The act of looking back changes the narrator, for his gaze is concentrated not on an earlier end but on a constantly unfolding middle.

Uncomfortable Memories

Memoirs that tackle childhood and adolescence are numerous, although they do not dominate the field. At their heart is a single refrain. Events, perhaps because of their *first*ness, have a way of overshadowing the growing consciousness of the child who experiences those events. Life deals; the child looks at its hand and rarely has time to consider what's dealt. The child is always imperiled: Mommy yells at Daddy that she's fed up with his womanizing and she wants him out, at which the child (and her little brother) can only bawl. The child does not understand the family dynamic; the child expresses it. The child is buffeted about by external forces and, though she feels much and wants to fight back, she doesn't. She can't. She's a victim. How often have I seen a memoirist feel overcome, in the initial stages of recall, by the heat, hurt, and isolation of childhood. Only later does the writer cool off and address who in the family the child was and the life which, lived out, became her destiny. That *addressing consciousness* is the adult writer. She begins to place the child into the larger story of the mother's neediness, the little brother's terror. To get to what is larger lies in summarizing events, where the themes of childhood can be constructed.

Summarizing and theme-finding, which, according to Frank McCourt, are "uncomfortable" tasks, come to writers after much conscious struggle. But there *is* a consciousness that inhabits our childhoods. It is, to be sure, a semiconsciousness about the family, the child's self, the pattern of events, which the child may perceive and hold to, even fleetingly. In my observation, that noticing is always there—call it one's sense of being, of being different. When the memoir writer mines that consciousness for what it knew, what it felt, she finds much that is wild. For the child, consciousness about what she is actually experiencing arrives like a snake in the grass, which darts onto the path, strikes quickly, and retracts into the thicket. For the adult, consciousness about what the self has experienced belongs to the *adult,* a serpent hunter who blazes his own trail and tracks the snake down. Most childhoods manifest themselves in the adult like this: first, the events themselves (for me, from my first memory at age five through a thousand more memories until age thirteen); and second, a consciousness about, or a shaped pattern of, those events, which continue to become *my* childhood throughout my life (for me, I began to recognize, even construct, the patterns of my early life, when I was in my late thirties).

Let's be clear about the forces involved in writing about childhood. At times, it is the child remembering (*wah, wah,* how I was wronged by selfish parents and a nasty brother). At other times, it is the adult remembering *inside of* and *for* the partially formed consciousness of the child (*I see, I see,* how my selfish parents were alcoholics and my brother's nastiness was his failed attempt to repudiate the family's disease).

And yet consciousness and chronology can get mystical. I have said that the mind which understands the child's growth in awareness of self and family does so after the fact: that mind was not in the child's day-to-day reaction to events, not part of the lizard-feeling little boy I was. And yet who else was feeling those things but the little boy I used to be? Who else was packing away those feelings but that long-ago self? I do not experience childhood after I'm grown. And yet I experience vestiges, bits and pieces of the child's helplessness, today as mine. Despite my partisanship, I cannot help or save or right that little boy now. I can only try to be honest about him now *for* then.

Geoffrey Wolff has paraphrased the famous Hemingway dictum about not falsifying the past quite well: "A writer's root charge is to distinguish what you really felt in the moment from the false sentiment of what you now believe you should have felt" (xxxiii). Through this porous border all memoir writers have stepped. To explore what we knew when we knew it. To hold Mother's passive-aggressive maybe-yes, maybe-no to the ambiguity of its time. To uproot our weedy latter-day self-inventions. But is any of this even possible? How does the author avoid the piling on, the grubbing for air among memories, the influence of dreams, the recollections reconfigured by religious and political bias, by love and loss, in order to see, let alone assess, original experience? Why even avoid it? No experience is pure; memory is all-corrupting. As historian John Lukacs notes in the context of writing history "accurately," what happened in the past is never separable from what we think happened. For Lukacs, history is an amalgam of fact and disputed fact: what's disputed may be the largest part of what's remembered.

WHEN I WAS A BOY in the 1950s, my obese authoritarian father favored me over my obese chaotic older brother; I was a different body type. How do I know I was favored? My father told me. I didn't know then the reason: that he and Steve were amped with self-loathing DNA that made each one catcall in the other that which each one hated looking at in the mirror. When my father overate, he yelled at Steve for overeating, too. Via therapy and writing, I came to know why I felt so bad for both men. But its seed— and the soil in which to root—was there. I knew *then* that a son-favoring father was the theme of my young life because I felt its beam on me cast the shadow of disapproval upon my brother. I could feel favoritism without knowing its cause. I could feel the pattern of favoritism without seeing its pulleys and wheels. And then, testament to its dominion, favoritism with my sons suddenly surfaced when I became a father—*shocking* and yet I shouldn't have been so shocked.

Which leaves the child-shaping memoirist where? Shouldering Virginia Woolf's "horrid labour" of making an expressive work of art. And contemplating three things about childhood and the memoirist. One, the writer who dramatizes emotions and events only from the child's perspective will appear innocent. Two, the writer who imposes the story of his self-consciousness in childhood upon what happened will appear intrusive. And three, the writer who directs how and to what degree that consciousness is revealed in the remembered and the remembering selves will appear adult. In all three perspectives, the memoirist (the writer *now*) cannot help but mix his consciousness today with the child's. And yet the memoirist must not let the child know what the memoirist knows, even though the competitive awareness of a self then and a self now is what makes conscious writing about childhood so dynamic.

5

Myth-Making in Memoir

How We Recollect

Psychologist John Kotre writes in his *White Gloves: How We Create Ourselves Through Memory* that our contemporary view of memory goes against the old notion that memories sit "inertly in our minds the way they do on an audiotape or the shelves of a library" (37). This view challenges centuries of memory mariners, among them Freud, who believed each remembrance is stored in toto and can be retrieved as such. The new idea (common sense, you might say) is that memories "are constantly refashioned" (37) by age and experience, but, more significantly, by the brain's storing and retrieving functions. Neurological activity forces memories to be updated without our say. Psychotherapy acts to move a troubled past from unexamined to exposed. Another catalyst, Kotre posits, is a remembering self, which is clear about its dual roles. One role is that of the archivist, who "guard[s] its original records and tr[ies] to keep them pristine." The other role is that of a writer-like self, who must "fashion a story about itself," "a story that some of us call the personal myth." Archivist and myth-maker establish "a comprehensive view of reality," whose coproductive authority seeks "to generate conviction about what it thinks is true" (116).

Kotre also suggests, as I've highlighted earlier, that we recall things differently during different life stages. While children's memories are general instead of specific and teenagers begin to detach themselves from experience and may be reflective, adults continually review their adolescent and young-adult intensities, shaping identity and the past anew. Adults and elders remember in different ways also. In Kotre's chapter "Memory in the Mature," the categories are flagged with purpose: "instrumental remembering," or the recollection of past achievements, is to "underwrite a sense of competence in the present" (175–76); "transmissive" remembering is "to pass on to others one's cultural heritage or personal wisdom" (176); "self-defining" memory is to make "not a precise account of what happened" but to find "a precise metaphor for what happened" (103–6); and "life review" is to come to terms with the past and to understand our essential themes (173–82).

Such designations remind us that memory serves the demands of the rememberer, who lives in the present. But these categories for the memoirist, in the throes of creating a book, are seldom if ever followed. How can they be? The act of drafting, akin to a two-year-old with a crayon, prompts the messiest details and exaggerations. All kinds of coloring ensue: my sisters *always,* no, *mostly,* no, *often,* no, *regularly* tormented me. What exactly should I recall, is one query. Another, perhaps more apt, is, what is my life now telling me *to* recall? We already know that our engagement with memory over time realigns the past. And yet we must learn as memoirists, through the years in which we work, that writing about the past realigns the memory. The question is, to what degree should such realignment be a part of the story. I sense a lot of reluctance in memoir writers, whether in published pieces or student drafts, even to pose this question to themselves in their work.

One reason for the reluctance to admit to memory's role is the extranarrative demands it places upon us as writers and readers. To remember, which for Kotre means "to generate conviction about what [the heart] thinks is true" (116), requires the writer to show himself *remembering*, that is, generating conviction about what is and is not true. It requires the memoirist to be as much tale-teller as rememberer, the latter a role that might slow down the tale considerably. Many memoirists, even those with a limited subject, are content to cozy their stories to autobiographical certainty—the past is over and done with and *here it is*—rather than push into the risky world of memoir, its Didion-like narrators full of essaying self-doubt.

Apropos of this is Annie Dillard's *An American Childhood,* which is usually regarded as a coming-of-age story, more autobiography than memoir, more what than who. The book is organized thematically as a series of semirelated topics: chapters on rocks, parents, Pittsburgh history, boys, a microscope, books, jokes, and so on. These topics are imposed on the material, and are collective more than individual in nature. On rare occasions, the idea of memory intrudes. But for Dillard, it's incidental. She writes—in exquisite prose—a crafted, memorializing remembrance, yet another halcyon tribute to the goodness of America in the fifties. Dillard avoids self-knowing, that is, *how* she has remembered herself and her family. The spade she used to dig out her childhood may have been difficult for her to wield. But that difficulty is not part of her story.

Does Dillard's 1987 autobiography seem passé in the new world of memoir? I'm not sure. Her tale-telling feels honest, reads beautifully. Dillard's certainty holds the past firmly in place. To psychologize would be unnecessary. Still, though the book resounds with first times, with discovery and innocence, there is no innocence lost—a tonal vantage that inhabits the best writing about youth. There is no purpose for Dillard now other than to tell us, this is my foundation, this is how it *was*. No revealing of the person to whom it happened. Many recent memoirists—at least in the direction their writing is taking—are challenging Dillard's reminiscence by asking, Why should any period of an author's life in a book be preserved, like a time capsule, in its context? If there is such a thing as the story of the past and the present has to accept it, why can't the past accept the present's intrusion into its time? The answer I hear is, it can. And so, more and more, we encounter authors who are writing time-loosed journeys, bringing the how-I-remember and the what-I-remember face to face. The point is to portray that which the memoirist sees when he looks in the mirror of the past: himself, living what he is remembering.

Mark Doty: The Altered Past

Few writers have used memory and their self-consciousness about it as skillfully as Mark Doty has in *Firebird* (1999). David Tuller noted, in his review, that "Doty's larger theme . . . is not the mundane miseries of childhood but the complex art of recollecting them—the ways in which we shape and transform our experiences into narratives that torment or sustain us."

In this marvelous story of Doty's early life, during which he alternated between repressing and asserting his artistic and, to a lesser extent, homoerotic self, Doty examines the nature of the self he keeps remembering. His goal is to understand how the self is made of a child's sticky ego and an adult's dissolving of that ego. He does so by identifying this self, which has been buried beneath his allegiances—family, friends, neighbors, culture, and his psychology. It *had* been buried while he was growing up. And it *has* been buried deeper as an adult. Doty grows the conflict between how he was the person he once was and how his memory held on to that person, until the act of memoir writing itself startles him awake.

One instance. In a perfect chapter called "Mikey," Doty tells of making friends at age seven in a new neighborhood in Tucson, where his father, an engineer, has been transferred to work in the missile industry. The time is the early 1960s, and his parents befriend families with children gaga for anything space-age—rockets, astronauts, a movie with Zsa Zsa Gabor as a Venusian queen. One Sunday, Doty's father takes his wife and his son to the silo site where he works so he and the mother can shoot handguns. Next, Doty recalls his friendship with Mikey, a neighbor boy who is retarded. "My mother explains it's not his fault that he's different, that he doesn't understand what other children do." Doty finds Mikey "interesting." He's pliable; he'll do anything you say. He's available, a completely social being. He's sweet; there's a "contagious happiness that's hard to miss." Because of all this "receptivity," Doty decides one day to give Mikey a haircut. What he first calls a trim goes bad, and the result is "a botched job." Mikey goes home, his mother sees it, and she comes to the Dotys' home, "in a quiet, contained rage," to lecture Mark about what he's done. She says, "Mikey trusts you, he doesn't know what you know, he can't do the things you can do, and you don't have the right to treat him like that, you don't have the right to treat him like he's nothing and cut his hair. It's not all right to treat a friend like that" (59–60).

Telling this story does a curious thing to Doty. The telling exposes two competing selves. "I am so ashamed," Doty writes (still in the past action but in present tense), "that I don't want to play with Mikey anymore, because I've done a bad thing." That's his child's voice. But, in the next sentence, something changes. "I've abused some power granted to me by accident" (60). That's the adult's voice. The voice that can't be kept at bay. The voice that interjects its judgment. And its understanding. A voice that knows now what the author did not know then. However, the child's voice rushes back to describe how Mikey and his mother return on Christmas Eve with a gift for Mark. The guilty boy has been forgiven, and he seems to have resolved the affair. (It's often good for the primacy of the story to keep the adult at least partly at bay.)

Christmas comes and goes. Now it's January, and Doty is arriving home from school. "There are police cars in the yard next door, and in our yard, and ambulances at Mikey's, crackly police radios, red lights twirling, and every now and then a siren letting out a little whoop as if it can't contain itself. People are standing around watching, the police officers keeping them at a distance, a big semicircle centered on Mikey's house, and now the neighbors are being interviewed, because Mikey's father has taken a gun and shot Mikey, and his other son, and his wife, and himself" (61). Recollected as dramatic shock (*in* memory and *for* reader), Doty has the child spit the story out. The sentences urge the child's compacting of experience into a single memory upon us; facts tumble out in a flash-forward (when Doty learns later that day what had happened) and in the breathy voice of the boy. The trauma of the day, backed by the shame of having once hurt this boy and been forgiven by him, is remembered in the child's voice: *the father killed them all.*

But, in the next instance, Doty sees himself peering in. "The boy I was, clutch of school papers in hand, seems unable to take in these events, or rather, all he can do is take them in, all eyes and ears, a kind of recording instrument unable to interpret." This *must* be the adult narrator who comes to the child's rescue—the storyteller's rescue, as it were. From here on, as if to calm the waters Doty himself has roiled, the adult narrator, directed by what Kotre calls a "self-defining memory," takes the reins. Doty labels the recording instrument (the action of his *present* memory) a "lunar vehicle," sent out to gather information. And as many times as Doty has launched this probe, trying to surveil the day of a neighborhood mass killing, the signal sent back returns only "bits and pieces of information" about the crime, Doty's "parents talking about it . . . when he's not supposed to hear" (61).

So far, he had contoured the incident with the adult's analysis so that the moment will make more sense for the child. Doty then takes another tack: to complete the story, he leaps an age hence. "Thirty-seven years later I'll have dinner with my father in a Tucson steakhouse, and we'll set to reminiscing." "He'll say, 'Remember when that woman killed her family?' And I'll say, 'Wasn't it the father? I remember it as the father,' but in fact I've got it wrong. And maybe that's why I can't remember the reaction of the boy I was to the erasure of a family, to the detonation of a parent's rage: I wasn't paying attention, exactly, to the facts of the story; I was revising it into something I could bear" (61–62).

How remarkable to add this accompanying voice: a future-flung narrator who reports that his father *will* say this and the author *will* answer. Doty's purpose? To say that the self-defining adult rememberer "got it wrong." That he's not as certain as he appears. But getting it wrong was also necessary for him to survive the shock, let alone live to tell it. Moreover, it is the way the child (who is still alive under the skin) remembers the experience: the adult, a mere delivery driver, supplies the words. What Doty writes is a memoir in which that adult authority is resized by a younger narrator who's come around to protect him, his adult scribe, with another version of the facts, another emotional truth. This is what Doty is so good at. In his hands, like those of Sylvia Fraser, disputatious narrators end up on the same side.

VARIANT TALES OF A NARRATOR, nesting in disparate moments of time, are among the most captivating memoirs being written these days. One such is Laurie Alberts's *Fault Line* (2004). As an adolescent and young woman, Alberts loved a man whom she also cheated on and eventually left. When he was found dead from exposure in 1994 twenty-five years after their affair (his alcoholism was a major factor), a picture of Alberts and him was discovered in his wallet. Her memoir describes their relationship, his illness, and her culpability for his demise. She includes several short but poignant chapters, which were inspired by the writing of the book itself. In these, she contrasts the life she has now with the life he didn't get to have. Alberts's story is more than her old lover's death and its effect on her. It's her ability to account for the effect that's so memorable—that, as she writes the past story, a present story emerges, tussles with, and transcends the past one. In the end, by being responsible to herself now, she honors the man's memory even more.

In Mark Doty's acknowledgments, he states that "the allegiance of this book is to memory; this is a past colored, arranged, and choreographed entirely by that transforming, idiosyncratic light. Any character here might well see things entirely differently. As my sister—bless her—put it, 'Well, the things you got wrong just make it that much more *you*'" (199). One wrong, now corrected, was the identity of the murderer in his neighbor's family.

Doty has named the memoir's bailiwick: its *allegiance to memory*. His acknowledgment echoes the "Mikey" chapter of *Firebird*, which shows, like Laurie Alberts's, an ability to dramatize the past and to account for the drama of what he's recollected. Such an awareness does not mean an author skates over history and culture—say, 1963 in Mississippi and a job registering voters just before Medgar Evers is killed; or 1994 in Los Angeles and being trapped for two days by the Northridge earthquake. That material, stage and drama, must be detailed. But the subject of a memoir is often the self in search of an earlier or a later self, who is found in the person the book gives birth to and whose awareness of past and present, in turn, becomes the focus.

6

The Writer as Archeologist

How Deep Do We Dig?

Memoirists often choose a life phase in which to position the singular relationship they are writing about. A phase, or distinct stage of development, is good because its limitation keeps the knight-errant author on track. And yet such a limitation can bedevil a writer, chiefly by unlocking other, equally important phases: If I was such a talented stock trader in the nineties, didn't my flair come from my father, who gambled his wages away when I was an adolescent? Which phase does the memoirist pursue: stock-trading days or adolescence? Again, I push the present-day rememberer: What is it about you *now* that's so interested in whatever stage you choose? Pressure from now may help unearth the best phase to explore, especially the unfinished ones that haunt us the most. And yet woe to the writer whose interlocking periods are stacked, as it were, like coffins on top of coffins. Woe, indeed, when the most recent coffin is buried the deepest.

Sue, one writer I've worked with, wants to tell the story of her marriage to a Christian fundamentalist and pot smoker who enthralled and abused her. She divorced him, has remarried, and is, needless to say, much happier. But she is not free of the trauma. To survive the marriage's worst moments she consciously put herself to sleep while it was happening. "This is so awful," she wrote in an e-mail, "that I'm choosing not to remember it. I will blot it out of my mind forever." When she began writing, she had no desire to recall her odious husband. Instead, she wrote about growing up Serbian in Milwaukee, recalling events perhaps *less* awful than the marriage. Sue describes her mother as "my role model for being a victim. She allowed my father to slap and kick her as well as my brother and me. We all tiptoed in terror around his temper. When he left—they divorced when I was nine—my maternal grandmother stepped in as resident ogre. My mother lived completely under the thumb of 'the master' as she called Grandma. My mother, in turn, controlled me with histrionic behavior, pouting, and the silent treatment—all under the guise of 'You can't do that because it will upset the master.'"

Co-generals, grandmother and mother, choked off Sue's self-esteem and caused her to seek a man cut from their domineering cloth. Marriage to him, she says, "couldn't have been avoided, given my upbringing." In her drafting of the book, the backstory ruled, harrowing in itself but, so she promised in teasing asides, not half as harrowing as living with the abusive pothead. Often, as she read excerpts to the group, Sue would erupt in crying jags; a paragraph recalling Elmer (she named him after Sinclair Lewis's character Elmer Gantry) would be met with her own choking gasps. At times she'd be unable to finish reading, so I would. For two years she persevered, detailing her family saga. Until one day, dismayed, she realized that after one hundred pages, she still hadn't got to the marriage. Those one hundred pages were, in her phrase, "just to set the scene."

I would caution Sue not to despair that the nine-year marriage remained in the wings. "Pay attention to what you *are* doing, though," I wrote her. "Your feelings now are dictating to you how you're going to write your book. The present writing about childhood is preparing you—like a friend—for the revelations of your marriage, which will come because you are building a number of buffers, painful ones themselves, before you can get to his barbarity. You are"—and here's a nugget personal narrators find particularly unwelcome—"writing about one part of your past so as *not* to write about another part, the part you really want to write about."

Aiding the fundamentalist's ex-wife are Sue's doggedness and humor, and a supportive group, some of whom are confessing their own marriage disasters. Ever so slowly, Sue is waking up from her slumber. As the book grows, she sees life with Elmer as pathetic and ridiculous and herself as a cagey survivor, somewhat more conscious than she had thought. The Elmer story is now off the ground, though it took a flock of stories about childhood to give it wing. Her deadening marriage, her most recent phase, has become the book. Elmer and she and their son are central and triangulated; her family—the female lot, still hungry ghosts—pokes through in choice flashbacks. Out from the under the thumb of drafting a memoir crawls a new structure, one Sue didn't know when she crawled in. It may now be the reverse: The latter-day marriage is what explains the long-ago crazy family.

Mary Karr: Excavating the Truth

Following Virginia Woolf's lead, thousands are breaking out of the autobiographical spell. The memoir writer, "the person to whom things happened," to whom it's never stopped happening, finds herself, in our free-swinging era, unleashed. She's angry. She's tired of being lied to. She's tired of lying to herself. She'll thump any head, including her own, that won't tell the truth. Such heart muscle belongs to one of the best writers of personal narrative in our age.

Mary Karr, in *The Liars' Club: A Memoir,* steers a very different course than Frank McCourt does in detailing a miserable childhood. Narrating misery's story in hundreds of brief episodes that span his early life is McCourt's tack. Karr's is different. Like a pointillist painting, her story and its two main phases reveal themselves in minutely descriptive, scenic detail. Chronicle is downplayed. Rather, Karr spotlights her childhood's most intense scenes, narrating them in clock time, and in long, dense chapters without space breaks. (The half-dozen or so events occur between ages six and eight, and at twenty-five when she returns home following her father's stroke; they also "occur" to the adult writer.) Each totalizing scene she calls "a single place in time." She opens with "My sharpest memory is of a single instant surrounded by dark," about which, one paragraph later, she writes, "it took three decades for that instant to unfreeze" (3). The scene is this: Karr's mother, who is already beset by problems in her marriage and the recent death of her own mother, goes berserk and burns the contents of the house in a huge bonfire in the backyard. Later, we see Karr's mother taken to a psychiatric hospital, but we don't know why she went crazy that day. That event is the mystery: to learn what prompted it is the reason Karr has written the memoir. The hyperdrama of her mother's breakdown requires fifteen pages of story, which Karr shifts, with seeming conscious intent, from past to present tense. The scene—Karr loves to make a scene in her stories—is unforgettable, best of show.

As I say, chronicle is secondary to the real-time event. Karr's lacquering of the detail, however, calls into question the accuracy of memory: how could she have remembered 1961 and 1963 (from her vantage thirty years later) with such Pentax clarity? Karr, as though she's being cross-examined by the memoir prosecutor, acknowledges that she's beset by this dilemma: she'll announce, *I remember it clearly*, and later confess, *that part has slipped out of my head.* (Early in chapter 1: "It was only over time that the panorama became animate" [4], which suggests a third way: the film of her youth is waiting to be developed.) Despite the method, it's difficult to accept how so many details would have been imprinted on her from ages six to eight. She retrieves closeups of people's actions from before she was born. For example, how did she know that "my grandmother was finishing an egg cream from the wrought-iron chair of a Lubbock drugstore when her insurance man stopped by" (316)? Her grandmother, whom she despised, died when Karr was a child. Where did the filigree trim of that instant come from? Or is this a memoir writer's license? Is it part and parcel of Karr's relentless need to ascribe sensuousness to every action? Is she, too, a member of the liars' club?

Karr's microscopic precision reveals something curious about memory, something I hadn't thought about until I lingered on some of her long and heavily brocaded passages. These appear when she's in sense-filled thrall to her mother's psychotic breakdown or to her first drink of burgundy wine and 7-Up at age eight, sipped from "Mother's bone-china cup":

> I'd heard her tell a hundred times how the monk who discovered champagne had likened it to drinking stars. Suddenly, that made sense. The wine and sparkly soda set my mouth tingling. I thought right off, *Drinking stars.* Whole galaxies could have been taking shape in there, for the taste was vast and particular at once. I'd taken too little a sip, though, and had to have another to see if the same small explosion happened. It did. I drank down some more. Besides its tasting good, the wine seemed to go down deep in me, not burning like it had before, but with a slow warmth. A few more sips set that warmth loose and rolling

down my limbs. I actually felt a light in my arms and legs where the alcohol was spreading. Something like a big sunflower was opening at the very center of my being, which image I must have read in a poem somewhere, for it came to me whole that way. (237)

A slight exaggeration—"heard her tell a hundred times"—begins the passage; it's in keeping with Karr's penchant to push the embellishing envelope in all her characters, including herself. Let's take her remembrance at face value. What she attests to—the "vast and particular" taste; the "small explosion"; the "not burning," and the "slow warmth"; the "light in my arms" and the "big sunflower" that blossomed inside her—is no doubt accurate to the first time. The first, so runs the claim, is the best. Yet, while this sip did have its onset, it has, certainly for her and her mother (that is, according to the family history of alcoholism in the memoir), been repeated a multitude of times. The sip's "firstness" happened in the moment. But it's also been revisited on subsequent drinks. (Doesn't the coffee I'm enjoying right now, while writing, share something with the ecstasy I felt the very first time I drank coffee, while writing? My current pleasure in drinking coffee is a ladder between its first rush and all those other rushes that have been added along the way, rungs to the moon.) Likewise, Karr's pleasure could have also occurred *now* while Karr was writing the book. She had a little nip. And by partaking, she accessed the feeling again, which is akin to accessing not the words that were there at her first sip but the words about that sip that have accumulated in her life since. I would contend that it is the subsequent drinks and the long-lived repetition of the drink's imprint, a sort of re-animation, that has created the feeling of "the first time" and presents it to the writer as authentic. Her accommodating memory has (not simply, mind you) layered or transmogrified or whatever into *ah, my first time.*

I'm not challenging Karr's honesty about the joy of her first spritzer. My point is to reveal the way a memory is multiplied by one's reenacting of that memory. First impressions may be pure, but they are also distilled as accumulating repetitions and an accumulating consciousness about them over time. I'm not advocating that every memoirist state this fact as a principle, once or often, in her book. That's too clinical, though Karr is a qualifier: "I doubtless thought" (146), "I've since come to know" (80), "That hits me funny, now" (256), "I recall no such scene" (257). Just to be aware of the overlaying nature of remembrance may help the memoirist sort out, à la Hemingway's dictum, the false sentiment of what happened from the real one. (The "whole truth," on which the court insists, is menacingly unfathomable: the whole truth is neither false nor true but is false *and* true.) Putting the past in the crosshairs may also force the memoirist to see that what she is dramatizing creates enigmas in her as a writer that readers pick up on, enjoy as well as question.

Finding Truth at Last

Here is one of the memoirist's many enigmas: if what I experienced was so vivid and yet so slow to materialize in memory, how do I construct the story to satisfy the reader's desire for narrative and how do I reveal the effects the construction of that narrative is having on me as I'm writing the book? Jovian narrative versus Jobian reflection. Such a commingling seems to be Karr's goal. Like a motet, she harmonizes the effect her traumas had on her during their time, the effect they have built in her up to now, and the effect it's having on her and the reader, who, in some sense, is inhabiting all this as Karr is in what feels like the writing-time of the book.

Despite my questions about her enhanced details, the touchstone of *The Liars' Club* is Karr's conflict between being accurate about and questioning her memory. I love this pitch-and-yaw in her work: while she ice picks the prose to absolute clarity, she also busts up the chronology, often bouncing from razor-sharp seeing to analyzing what she has seen. As we read, we are unaware of her research methods—her superrealist recall; her facility with metaphor; her use of journals, tapes, and photos; her having shown drafts to her mother and sister for their input—plus there's no question she was the Family Watcher (something I say to those pulled to write memoir: you were as much assigned the observer role in the family, as you were a natural at it). In sum, we sense that all these things have weighed on our teller and produced not just the person who had to write this book but the tenacity to see it through. Lest we forget, such tenacity is nine-tenths of talent.

Honesty haunts the book's events in other ways, such as the forced oral copulation that Karr experienced when she was eight. This rape scene—etched in eight graphic pages—is as memorable as any incident in *The Liars' Club*. Again, how can the author recall such detail? Unlike the chronic, almost daily trauma of Sylvia Fraser's abuse, Karr's episode is "only" one instant and its recollection has, apparently, not led to the kind of dissociation that caused Fraser to split. Whereas the first-sip-of-the-spritzer scene is cued in Karr's memory by her later drinking, the rape is cued by a number of coproductive circumstances. She writes, "More nights scrolled past and days so gray and grainy that not one stands unblurred from any other, till I get sick one day and the grown man who allegedly comes to care for me winds up putting his dick in my eight-year-old mouth. In fact, the whole blank winter sort of gathers around that incident like a storm cloud getting dense and heavy" (239). The "reason" this attack happens is that Karr's age and demeanor as well as her family's antichild attitudes conspire toward and ripen in this moment: Her mother goes out a lot and drinks and hires babysitters; her mother trusts the wrong kind of men to watch Mary while she's out; Mary loves to describe her fantasies about characters in books to people who watch her; Mary is also adept at gaining the trust of adults with her ability to describe and share what she's read. Moreover, she's good at getting stuck between the man's "seduction" and her ability to feel that what she's experiencing is no different from a tender moment a book portrays. Even at eight, Karr's mind is occupied with sexual images—thoughts about fucking and penises that occur to her (is she, was she, attracting him? now? then?) as he approaches.

Karr laces together present awareness and memory, child and adult voices, innocent imagining and wise reimagining. Her rendering of what she's resurrecting—how it happens once and all over again—is what I mean by honesty. This is *not* a pure chronology of what the child would have experienced, day in, day out, as if that were even possible. Instead, it's an emotional tableau of the multisensory, the transtemporal, which nevertheless still ends in the man's ejaculation and Karr's vomiting.

The scene feels climactic, but it's also preparatory, making possible the final scene, one equally appalling. The writer's drama also continues, that is, the *effort* it takes to access the past. The end emerges for her as a memoirist after she has begun to attend to the rape and other "single instants" with the help of a professional. She tells us this fact during the final section: at age twenty-five (in 1980), Karr was seeing a therapist whose advice on how to get her mother to confess to her past travails Karr uses to flush out the demons of her family's lunacy. It is the memoir's pivotal and most revealing self-disclosure: when she has to connect herself at twenty-five to herself ages six to eight as well as connect those ages to herself, the grown-up author writing now.

To connect is to resolve.

Karr's laboring to remember guides the book's conclusion. The final ten pages, set in 1980, bring her mother's motives to account—why she went berserk that night in 1961, leading to her institutionalization and to Karr's lifelong need to know why. The memoir loops to before the story's beginning. There Karr finds her mother's original sin—the fact that after her first "marriage" at fifteen and after the birth of two children, those children were stolen from her by her husband and her husband's mother. What was worse was once Karr's mother found them, brandishing the legal paperwork that guaranteed those kids were hers, and hers to take back, she decided not to because she knew she had no way of caring for them.

John Gardner, in *The Art of Fiction,* uses the term *profluence* to define the reader's sense of getting somewhere in a story. Karr gets somewhere because she is *emotionally* profluent throughout the book. Of her mother's madness, shame (her child's judgment) gives way to sympathy (her adult response) over time. Interacting at different paces, these conflicting emotions eventually run their course, a ravine hollowed out by seasons of earth-loosening rain. What empties Karr empties her parents as well.

No doubt the adult's closure salved the child's wound. And yet, even at the end, Karr is still haunted. The book's closing image— a dream of heaven, "some luminous womb," where death may carry her "without effort till the distant shapes grow brighter and more familiar, till all your beloveds hover before you, their lit arms held out in welcome" (320)—feels mystically incomplete, despite all the erupted fact of memory. Childhood, girlhood, adulthood, therapy in her twenties, recollecting the hurt for another fifteen years—and only then, in medias res, to present it all to her sister, her mother, her father, so they too might face the family illness? Or not. A memoirist in the family, a doomsayer, a savior.

TRADITIONAL BOOK FORMS are on a never-ending circuit, lecturing their adopters. The novel tells the novelist to be imaginative with narrative and scene; the poem tells the poet to merge sound and sense in illumined brevity. For generations, the autobiography has told its author that his life should glow with the author's profession, ideas, accomplishments; it should follow a life path that's eminent and consequential; it should rely on summary and be publicly tactful. The autobiographer should also be finished with life. What's done is done. Decisions now are irrelevant. The life is prior to the writing.

I don't think the memoir is telling the memoirist what to do. At least not yet. Rather, the memoirist is doing all the talking. Be flexible, she says, be inclusive, be not merely chronological and novelistic, be disruptive, be yourself. At sixty-four, Judith Moore wrote the tale of her lifelong struggle with obesity in *Fat Girl: A True Story*. For the most part, the book stays in childhood and adolescence. Why did it take her so long to tell this tale? Was the shame so great that it had to be repressed, then found, then filtered through memory as Mary Karr's did? Perhaps she needed years. Perhaps she waited for the memoir form to evolve or the form waited for Moore to be proactive. Was it even about shame?

We know some of how she dealt with her memories because her opening three chapters position her as a rememberer: Moore's a fat woman whose present unhappiness triggers the story of how she became the person she's always been. Not transformed into fat, but chubby and burdened and less than from the get-go. "I am on a diet," she writes in rhapsodic minimalist prose. "I am almost always on a diet. I am trying to get rid of pounds of my waddling self. I am always trying to get rid of pounds of myself" (7). Moore says that the weight she has always tried to get rid of, she cannot, not at her age. She's given up, so she gives in. She lingers for her pleasure and ours on the taste of a two-handed restaurant cheeseburger with pickle-mayo-mustard-tomato-lettuce, the bun soggy, the bites full-mouthed. She refuses to look into the mirror of shame. Rather, she suggests that shame is the viewer's vice. It is our media-induced projection onto her of an impossibly universal thinness, a fascistic body clone, that says the fault is hers, *hers* alone. Moore rejects it. Her "fat girl" is today's "fat woman," still "waddling" with the stretch marks of childhood. She knows what we don't want her to tell us, and then she tells us. The scraping sound of her bulging thighs. The humid sweat of her stomach folds. Without sorrow or guilt. Like the memoir form, Moore accedes to no one's wishes but her own.

7

Sudden Memoir (1)

No Time to Reflect

I call the memoir that examines a most recent life phase *sudden memoir*. A memoir of a recent event avoids the hindsight of age and captures something before memory can edit it. Sudden memoir is as daring as it is histrionic: listen, this just happened to me; you've got to hear about it as much as I've got to tell it to you. (Down this lane, we find those who are enthroned for the day by CNN: think freed West Virginia miner or runaway bride. These as-told-to books are initiated by greedy publishers, not daring authors, and are not part of this study.) Sudden memoir of the literary sort helps the writer cope, get through, get past. The just-completed can be anything: endurance (a medical intern's resident year), failure (one day blowing the kid's college fund at the racetrack), life change (last summer—and love—in Andalusia). Memoirs like Anatole Broyard's *Intoxicated by My Illness* (1992) and Harold Brodkey's *This Wild Darkness: The Story of My Death* (published the year he died, 1996) brood upon the stingy light of an illness. Often called "pathography," such books entwine belligerent regret with beatific farewell.

Again, it is the memoirist—the charging rhinoceros—who wants his say now. Why so soon a reckoning? Why not wait for things to settle down, sort themselves out? Answer these with another question. Where is it written that memoir needs a Jurassic crawl of time to pass for the writing to be honest and affecting, even necessary? Such are the prejudices of psychotherapy, which, applied to literary forms, run counter to the instincts of authors. When the memoirist headlines a recent drama, she is, in large part, freed from the tyranny of memory. We've already seen the kind of tyranny that can accrue once a "sufficient" amount of years has passed: the writer is deluged by memories and must contend with the muck underfoot. Sudden memoir seeks no such end. The form is an assault on the present by the present and its colleague, an almost current past. No alternative is possible: the story commands us to write it as a way of sentencing it to memory.

I HAVE TWO PHOTOGRAPHS. One is of my brothers and me sitting in an Adirondack love seat, our newest brother, Jeff, in the middle between my older brother, Steve, and me. It is 1956, the place, our grandmother's backyard in Rockford, Illinois. Short sleeves and dungarees say summer. Jeff sits up, a little Buddha, though he seems still wobbly at fifteen months. I'm wearing white moccasins, a vestige of my Indian period, when, at six, anything beaded and feathered delighted me. At nine, Steve is beginning to reveal the weight that would gather on him the rest of his life: fat and heart disease would cause his death thirty-three years later. What I see in the picture—perhaps you can hear it in my memorializing description—is the future we have lived out, emanating from this captive moment. (Of course, were I to show you the photo, *you* couldn't see that element; I would have to put it into memoir.) We all share this tendency: to read the future as it exhales from a remote past, the intervening time in which we have lived.

The other photograph I have is of Jeff in Atlanta, in 1999, forty-three years later. The photo reveals he has a filled-out, middle-aged body, a balding dome, a plain shirt and quick-tied tie, the professional countenance of a program manager with the Georgia Department of Natural Resources. A recent event, though, stalks the picture: my brother is freshly divorced. The photo, taken by his daughter, betrays that haggard, liberated stare. I can't view the shot without seeing, *oh, yes, that's the summer just after he and Diane split*. The picture engages sympathies in me that are far different from those in the photo from 1956.

The advantage of the 1999 photo to the memoirist (me, today) is that there's less of an intractable future in it. There *is* an intractable and buried past, but not a future. How surprising! The photographs, talking to me now, have the power to make apparent my experience of time. In 1956, life is ahead of us. I don't see my mother in the photo, though I'm sure she took the picture, dressed us in matching outfits, and arranged us in protective positions on either side of our little brother. We three brothers possess few of the cuts and bruises of the Larson dysfunction (too highfalutin a word, no doubt), although on the genetic-fatalistic level some prophecy is evident—as I say, Steve is showing his fat, its discomfort, its enslavement. (I, who didn't suffer weight gain, wear the absence of his weight upon me, which may be just as characterizing.) But notice: there's some indifference on Jeff's face. He's stuck between us. He's six years younger and seems, though our arms enclose him gently, afraid that we will squish him. Steve and I would have begun annoying him at that age already. Jeff would later describe it as torture and claim that Steve and I participated with equal hunger, though I remember Steve being the bastard, not me. That sibling future is tilted into the photo. Jeff looks (or do I read this in?) beleaguered, perhaps by his daemon—an attendant power or spirit, guiding him within, expecting trouble.

By 1999, a life beyond his brothers' influence has made him. He is past the deaths of our parents and of Steve. And he is fully ensconced in the chaos he knew just before and during the divorce. Following his wife's affair and her announcement that she wanted out, following her daring afternoon liaisons with the lover, Jeff would call or e-mail me at times, frantic. He was livid about his wife's flaunting her sexual freedom; he didn't think he could survive as an absent father; he was agonized by being unable to tuck the kids into bed at night. And, six months later, the strangest bit of all: Having been rejected by the man whom she left Jeff for, she came back to him, my brother. He phoned me while she was in his bed, and during the call, pretended to me that she wasn't there, although I learned later he was terrified that in his vulnerability he would take her back when he shouldn't, though it might be good for the kids. All that the solitary photo of him speaks to. It demands my attention. It isolates his trauma. It exudes the pain of that ruinous year and their ongoing mutual hatred, even down to now. By contrast, in 1956, the family memory is an artifact; it lacks the urgency of the person who has just lived it.

Were I to write a memoir of my relationship with my older brother, it would be based in the reconstituted memory of our childhood (we battled when young but became close in adulthood) alongside his tragic death (and its effect on my mother), leaving behind a wife and a newborn child. The suddenness in that memoir would lie in my retrieving our history for my emotional aims now. Even with those present feelings, the book would touch upon a distant past, which has been buried and processed and mythologized over many years, and would take a lot of digging to disinter.

Were I to write a memoir of my relationship with my younger brother, it would be based in our still-settling emotions—his for himself and mine for us. In the last six years, the one honest story I could tell about him and me is about how divorce and loneliness are reshaping his character and also bringing us closer. Once he sought my advice, and I was able to offer some by recalling the clamp of my own divorce, we have matured as brothers. Still another reason would be to open up and feel the distress about my failed marriage, the loss of all romantic expectation about my childhood and adult families.

To write sudden memoir, I resist the accumulation of any *more* time upon my story. I unleash the narrator, who, in shaping the tale up to and including last night, is far different from the narrator who rummages through the sea chest, looking for the mythic self. Sudden memoir is sword and shield against my epic-making self, who, as John Kotre notes, will distort whatever he needs to so "the speeds get faster, the fish get bigger, the Depression gets tougher" (117).

Kathryn Harrison: In Immediate Peril

Consider Kathryn Harrison's necessarily short *The Mother Knot: A Memoir* (2004). It's a one-themed book: a resentful daughter (Harrison), who carries her dead mother's judgment of her, must resolve that judgment before it ruins her. It's sudden because Harrison has just lived through the story's culminating crisis, scattering her mother's ashes. At times the memoir's narrative has a perilous immediacy; other times it's discursive. She must have written the sixteen-thousand-three-hundred-word story during the crisis and in late 2003, following a traumatic episode with one of her children in fall 2002 and the ashes-scattering climax, seven months later, in spring 2003. The book opens with the writer clinging to a recent memory when she was nursing her youngest daughter; this is her last child, so breast-feeding is irrevocably gone. When her son has a severe asthma attack, Harrison panics.

Something in her manic devotion to nursing and to her children's safety renews her depression, throwing her back to an episode four years earlier when she was hospitalized for a suicide attempt. She starts examining why she feels so traumatized by her own protective instincts.

A successful writer, whose *The Kiss: A Memoir* (1997) was a major advance in the rise of memoir, Harrison carries a poisonous family history. She's already told the world about her "affair" with her father. Worse, she's knotted up by a "sadist" (28)—so labeled by Harrison's analyst—for a mother. This woman tossed away her husband, Harrison's father, and, soon after, unloaded Kathryn on her grandparents. The author's earliest memory of her mother is rejection, "pushing me out of her lap." "'Get off,' she said. 'You're too heavy'" (55). Before dumping her, the mother put Harrison on a diet when she was seven, forcing her to drink skim instead of whole milk. Headstrong Harrison forever more refuses whole milk and, when she is a teenager, her anorexia begins. "I was the girl," she writes, "who loved and hated her mother in equal measure, whose longing was obvious and whose rage had always been concealed, even—especially—from herself" (8). The consequences of her rage live on. Harrison has an "irresistible" (75) need to cut herself, and she continues to fall into obsessions of exercise and not eating. A year before the birth of her third child, Harrison was hospitalized with depression. Now she is starving and her doctor tells her that she's a few days or a few pounds from again being hospitalized and, this time, force-fed.

The breakthrough comes during a session with her psychiatrist. She writes, "I'd heard myself speak what I hadn't yet thought" (49). She knows that she's a good parent to her kids, unstressed and positive, but she's terrified that what's unresolved in her has unloosed her son's illness. His asthma, she thinks, is the asthma she once had as a child. It strikes her that her self-mutilation and depression are centered on her mother's inability to love her. She has to extricate herself from this woman who is buried inside, a dybbuk, pulling her under via starvation and self-loathing so mother and daughter can be dead together. Harrison decides to act: she has her mother's body disinterred, cremated, and flown to New York, where she lives. There she'll disperse Mom and the curse into the ocean.

Harrison's liberation from this specter is poignant and convulsive. In the final chapter, roughly one-fifth of the whole, she juxtaposes four different times. There is the current action of a March 2003 afternoon at the ocean's edge where she has brought the ashes; there is the twenty-year-old conversation with her dying mother, who told her that after she was gone she, Kathryn, would be very angry with her; there is the memory of a walk she and her mother took a few years before that talk, when her mother introduced her to the power and immensity of the sea; and there is Harrison's wedding, at which her mother-in-law pointed out that Harrison's mother was absent, a comment which nearly ruined the day. Harrison's mother's death and her need to let go interlace these memories and events. In the end, Harrison's exorcism is cathartic. I was reminded of the therapist John Bradshaw's admonition to anyone terrorized by his or her (family) demons: "The first thing you have to do is to feel as bad as you feel." Harrison initiates the descent, on a cold spring afternoon at the seashore, where memories of her mother's cruelty coalesce. At the same time, she activates those emotions by dumping the ashes and freeing herself. It's paradoxical. While it may seem that much of what happens in this final chapter is recalled, the present-forced, ritualized purging of the demon—"to take arms against a sea of troubles, / And by opposing end them?"—has resolvent power. Sudden memoir is the most useful memoir there is.

Is there a better time in which to feel how bad one feels than during or in the immediate wake of a trauma? It may not be possible, physically, psychologically, to feel that bad *during*. And yet what is "during" anyway? For Harrison, for any of us, it takes our childhoods and adulthoods to collect and thicken our resentments. And yet how much is lost to time? Had Harrison waited five or ten or twenty years until she wrote *The Mother Knot* (certainly an option), how radically different that memoir would have been—detached, philosophic, processed.

One way *The Mother Knot* satisfies us is its equivalency to a felt trauma: it's a tale short on pages but long on intensity. It resists enlargement, the Churchillian pull to overpuff the past. It also has a ferocity about it, summoned to purpose: either I'm going to get through this now or it's going to kill me. For Harrison, it's clear that if she doesn't untie the knot with Mom, then, as her analyst tells her, she will *re-mother* the emotional crime in herself. "You haven't fucked [the children] up, but you're fucking yourself up! You're destroying yourself, and that will fuck up your children! It will fuck up everyone you love" (43)! (The analyst's blue hollering, Harrison says, is unusual.) Added to the trauma of letting her mother go, the writing of this sudden memoir is a second trauma, an aftershock. Twin screams of the soul could not have been easy to endure. Such are the stakes. But such, too, is the energy of closure, the surprise of survival. You may think you may not survive, but you do because the writing, like oxygen, keeps you going.

ONE MEMOIRIST I KNOW (her name is Kim) wants to narrate the story of how she cared for her husband, at home, by herself, as he died of amyotrophic lateral sclerosis, or ALS, Lou Gehrig's disease. But she's avoiding the chronological story: one day, ten years ago, he slurred his speech: and then, and then, and then he died in 2000. Kim took my memoir class because, she writes in an e-mail, "I felt that the horror and the pain had gone their separate ways; the journey was over; and, consequently, I was detached enough to write about it. I almost immediately realized that I was mistaken." She couldn't get much of it done at all. But then something happened during the course that has allowed her to tell some of the story of how she endured her husband's wasting and paralysis. She begins the tale offstage: her closest friend, Jayne, has just fallen in love with a man and suddenly loses him: he has a heart attack while driving and dies in the wreck. Consoling Jayne, Kim is thrown back to the long-term caretaker role she had with her husband. This, in turn, brings back his five-year battle as well as their time together before the disease. Consoling Jayne also uncoils her first real *telling* of the loss, "to simultaneously walk with death and hold onto life." At last, feeling comfortable with Jayne, who "wanted me to talk to her about death and dying, I was able to recount the experience to her and then to write about it. By wholly revisiting and revealing my experience and my feelings, by putting them into words, I unleashed my grief."

What is sudden is that there's no telling how the memory will return. Serendipity or fate, take your pick. At first the writer is witness. She sees in one current event or phase an earlier event or phase that vies for equal time, equal expression. Kathryn Harrison's fixation on her children unblocks her lifelong fixation on her mother. For Kim, the slow dying of one beloved man is necessary to understand the sudden dying of another. Once awake, the writer exerts control. She decides to get to the deeper past as it makes itself known in the recent past, writes it in thrall to whatever is activating memory to speak now.

A few pages into Beverly Lowry's *Crossed Over: A Murder, a Memoir* (1992), we know that the author's parents have died and that her seventeen-year-old son Peter has been killed in a freakish accident. She writes, "The death of parents is never easy, but your child's death, pure and simple, puts you under. Sometimes, it seems, for good." Emotionally lost, Lowry is drawn to the case of Karla Faye Tucker, a young Houston woman who admitted to "having killed two people, but who then went home and boasted to her rowdy friends about having done it" (3). Tucker and two male accomplices were sentenced to death. (She would eventually be executed in 1998, Texas governor George W. Bush rejecting her appeal even though Tucker had become a Christian.) The vulnerable Lowry is pulled into Tucker's psyche, her remorse and cruelty; the writer runs only on association. "I am trying to make connections . . . to illuminate or at least make a case for a plausible narrative. I am trying to get the whole of it to come into focus" (2). One way to make sense of the senseless is to connect the randomness of her son's death to the randomness of the deaths of those Tucker murdered. Lowry soon realizes that "if Peter hadn't been killed, I would not have made the first trip up to see Karla Faye" (4). But, as she gets close to Tucker on Death Row, she admonishes herself, "You don't want to get involved with another young person who will die" (13). Lowry finds herself bonding with the murderess in ways, some motherly, some desperate, she was bonded with her son. The effect disturbs and captivates, author and reader. In Lowry's feelings for Tucker lies the meaning. Somehow this killer (soon to be gone herself) is the living embodiment of death, a persona to whom Lowry can talk as though she, Karla, were her dead son. Lowry's memoir records how grief *removes* her—to where, for what purpose, she has no idea. The longest road she travels is this: her unlikely compassion for Tucker gives her reason to live while the death of her son and the deaths of Tucker's victims (children to other parents) take the reason away.

8

Sudden Memoir (2)

Dave Eggers: A Trauma (Kind of) Resolved

Though the sudden memoir is still a fledgling, the best one I know of, a thematic kin to *The Mother Knot,* is Dave Eggers's *A Heart-breaking Work of Staggering Genius* (2000). Eggers's memoir is about the coterminous deaths of his parents and the abrupt change the author faces in his tidy life because he now must raise his eight-year-old brother. While Harrison's ultrathin volume is unidimensionally intense and directionally certain, Eggers's bardic yawp is self-indulgent and artful as well as confused and conflicted about what he thinks his story is or should or might be but can't quite figure out, despite himself. Both stories share an ending: the dispersal of a parent's cremains. Both stories also take on the great parental attachment adult children suffer, which directs them to ultimately purge that attachment.

How Eggers deconstructs the suddenness of his trauma is wholly original. I think I can explain it (or, as Eggers's Gen-Xers would

say-ask, I think I can *kind of* explain it?). He begins (but not before he mocks the memoir form with forty-plus pages of rules,
suggestions, acknowledgments, flowchart, a financial reckoning
of his advance, a drawing of a stapler—the whole desultory feat,
he instructs us, we can skip) with the cancer deaths of his parents,
his father predeceasing his mother by five weeks. Their departures
are portrayed differently: the mother's anguish during her final days
is dramatized while the father's is shown piecemeal, distant and
unfelt. The twenty-one-year-old Eggers fits their dying into the
quotidian regime he, his older sister Beth, and his eight-year-old
brother Christopher, or Toph, are living. Unlike parents who lose
their children, children don't stop their lives to mourn when parents die. They go on, comically, blindly—unfazed by grief, so it
seems. Months later, Toph says he's starting to forget them. Eggers gets out the photo albums to make sure his brother doesn't.
"Unfazed by grief" may be too pat. For the young, grief has not
possessed them yet. It is festering in the subconscious, as Eggers
will learn many station stops down the road.

Thus, it's no surprise to find sudden death sidelined by a sudden new life once the siblings move from Chicago to Berkeley.
There, while his sister studies law, Eggers manages Toph. (The
action of the memoir—it all *feels* sudden, *feels* yesterday—takes
place mostly in the Bay Area and covers Eggers's early twenties
and Toph's adolescence.) As the go-to parent, wisenheimer Eggers
must get Toph to school, be at home when he comes back, get
him to eat decent food and not just junk (which both crave and
consume), live on a budget, and find the right sitter (the biggest
hassle for the gonadal author). Most of what Eggers wants is to
partake of things *his* age—goof off with his buddies, spend time
at a magazine for which he adds his graphic-design talent, start a
cultural stir with his ideas, whose sybaritic proportions remind
us of Andy Warhol's Factory. To be a parent when biology and all
temptation are telling him to socialize and stay out at night makes

for much paternalistic comedy. Eggers is a libertine dad. He and Toph are moonwalkers: they play Frisbee, spend hours sock-sliding in their new house, go wild at a beach picnic. For the first half of the book Eggers freewheels. He follows tangents in the life and in the narrative; he riffs on the Berkeley-ness of Berkeley; he fantasizes about single moms he meets at PTA. We sense his resisting the notion that a memoir—like his and his brother's lives—have a goal. We also sense his goallessness cannot be sustained. As loose as he is, Eggers is also paranoid.

Eggers (kind of) realizes that what he's doing to/for Toph is misguided and selfish: bad things may result. He doesn't just wake up to this fact or start acting more responsibly (though he does report real and imagined social pressures that insist he shape up). Once the predictability of parenting and dating get to him, he escapes to Alt Youth Cult and starts sinking into pop culture. Alt Youth Cult is the site of TV-addicted twenty-somethings (pre-Internet, pre-iPod), where what is real is definitely what is mediated. This is the wired-up dystopia foretold by Haskell Wexler, whose film *Medium Cool* (1969) exposed how televised images care nothing for the content of what they cover. It is the land of how-will-it-play-on-camera. Nowadays medium cool is ubiquitous and attractive to the collective mind. Eggers leaps onboard, replacing the *I* of his narration with *we*. In such *we*-ness, little individual gets in. Every act is project-based—which, for Eggers, is blessedly impersonal. He's got enough *personal* going on with Toph. To be up with Alt Youth Cult is to be away from the shitty home life. Eggers would like to be a total slacker, but, going home every night, he's reminded of his parents' absence, his inconsistencies as a surrogate father.

At the heart of Alt Youth Cult is MTV's *The Real World,* a program, premiering in 1992, about seven people who move in together in a New York apartment. The idea of *The Real World* (which memoir shares) is to make celebrities out of nobodies. How? By filming them. Doing what? Interacting, chilling, watching MTV, their "real" lives modeling product-focused behavior. Many we-landers want in. But only a few make it: not just any nobody is videoworthy. Eggers, who with his buddies has started a magazine called *Might*, decides, as a story idea, to audition for *The Real World*. He makes a wacky audition tape and gets the call. The interview with an MTV·producer is offered in the book as a "transcript" of their Q-and-A. Today we know *The Real World* as the dark seed of what's become "reality TV," or as an eleven-year-old girl more accurately named it, "fake reality TV." It's a form that puts *us* on as we put *it* on. So here, I digress to Eggers's method, which we might term "fake memoir." During much of the book (recall his arch preface), Eggers writes "imagined" episodes. He imagines that his mother dies in a way that's easier on *him;* he imagines getting home late one night from a date to find the babysitter killing Toph; he imagines Toph breaking "out of character" and lecturing *him* about parental duty. The imagined life is part of the life Eggers narrates, not only for humor but also for relief from his self-doubt as a parent.

So Eggers begins putting on for the MTV interviewer. He says he can't help it: he's "feeling a format change coming, one where quotation marks fall away and a simple interview turns into something else, something *entirely so much more*" (184). There follows, for fifty brilliant pages, a set of orchestral variations on "real" and "faked" self-disclosure. Much of what he and the female interviewer discuss is, we assume, factual: hometown, childhood, family, friends. Then, to jar it loose from fact, Eggers cracks the mask and has the woman supply, in her voice, *his* guilty conscience.

> *So tell me something: This isn't really a transcript of the interview, is it?*
> No.
> *It's not much like the actual interview at all, is it?*

Not that much, no.

This is a device, this interview style. Manufactured and fake.

It is.

It's a good device, though. Kind of a catchall for a bunch of anecdotes that would be too awkward to force together otherwise.

Yes. (196–97)

The interview usurped, Eggers confronts what's eating him. She asks, isn't it hard raising your brother? Yes, it's hard; it's very hard, he says. He opens up. And your mother? And your father? He opens up about them, too, and their dying. At last, a book that's been pretending to be a memoir suddenly becomes one— the irrepressible kind in which you begin to utter truths, truths that have been growing weedlike within because you've been so afraid that your telling them will hurt. Eggers remembers his parents' funerals, their cremations, the fact that their cremains are still in transit; who they were (father: raging alcoholic; mother: piteous martyr); details of their cancer-ridden final days. This is what we've been waiting for—the pus dome rising from the untended wound—the latent and richest material of his life. The interview segment interplays his parents' lives and deaths against Eggers having barely begun to examine/mourn their loss; which, in turn, triggers another interplay between the surprise of his confessions and the fact that he's been ducking his memories; which, turning again, brings him fully into his backwards-dragging present where what he's been trying to write has been leading him all along.

WHAT EGGERS HAS DONE—or, better, what the writing has done to Eggers—is to dramatize his discovery of his book's center while it's happening to him in a book he's writing that he finds must include the conditions under which that discovery can take place so that as he's writing the book the discovery will occur. Not what the autobiographer had in mind.

Why, we wonder, doesn't Eggers just tell us what's on his mind? Why must he craft a device in the context of playing to the media? The reason is clarified once he admits that his generation, in trying to get on TV any way they can, wants "to prove to all and ourselves that we are real, that we like everyone else simply want our lives on tape, proven, feel that what we are doing only becomes real once it has been entered into the record" (246). How curious! To be on *The Real World* would be an experience, though obviously faked, which would feel "real" to those involved and "real" to those watching it. Because it's been recorded. Because recorded life is that much richer than a life merely being lived. Not much different from what the memoirist wants.

In the end, *The Real World* rejects Eggers as a cast member. Too bad. But for readers, it's a good thing: the form he's writing is really starting to bear fruit. For example: At first, we think that since his interview is videotaped, it won't lie. But in turning the videotaped interview into a lie, he's able to say something larger. *Any* means by which we record our lives is subject to question. Memoir writing itself gives Eggers the means to create and destroy, to make a duplicitous memoir as his record. Which is also saying something profound about Generation X. Their lesson is to learn for themselves and to show the rest of us how much contemporary existence is mediated. By TV. By us. Even by memoir. Such is the thrust of the memoir form in the hands of contemporary innovators like Eggers and Geoff Dyer and Lauren Slater: To come across as "real" to readers, one's potentially true story must be understood—and dramatized—as one's potentially faked story. Much as the "reality TV" format renders actual life, at the same time its presentation succeeds in falsifying that life.

Once Eggers has had his fun deceiving us, he starts finding himself. The tack resonates with most readers. Think of the deceiver, coyote, hero of native American folk tales, or of Picasso's famous line, "Art is a lie that tells the truth." To play tricks with perception is to get people to pay attention to how they perceive. The artist instructs our response to his art. Once Eggers sabotages the conversation from MTV job interview to Augustinian confession, his truth-telling voice finds its stride, even as it mocks its content and stages its form. At last, his family tragedy starts getting "on the record," in a (kind of) Eggers-ese. The trickster gets to memoir by undermining the form. Which is (I trust you're getting the picture) part of where the form is calling from.

Eggers's ironic voice ping-pongs between hyperfree and hyperresponsible. He writes with genuine sarcasm and genuine emotion. The more he worries about his lifestyle, the more he yields to that lifestyle; the more he's conscious of being playful, the more serious he becomes. Of course, writing in the present tense, as he does, activates the now. At the same time, the present tense mirrors the inextinguishable, which we might call the in-time tense of TV. Television is on right now, which is no different from life, which is also on right now, which is no different from a sudden memoir, which is the *illusion,* in present tense, that it's on right now or, at least, on very recently. Such is Eggers's zing, his hot-wiredness. As one blogger described it, "His prose is nothing if not a dance performed to keep life going" (Keefe). This is key. By making his commentary on what happened as central *as* what happened, Eggers adds a metanarrative. Metanarrating may be the only way a memoir can get written if the memoir's self-awakened subject is *how do I write one.*

In an interview, Eggers described the importance of an activating style. "On the one hand, you are so completely bewildered that something so surreal and incomprehensible could happen [the death of his parents]. At the same time, suddenly the limitations or hesitations that you might have imposed on yourself fall away. There's a weird, optimistic recklessness that could easily be construed as nihilism but is really the opposite. You see that there is a beginning and an end and that you have only a certain amount of time to act. And you want to get started" (Lyall).

The more bewildered Eggers was, the more he had to write out that bewilderment, trust it to yield direction. It's a matter of energy, too: memoir is an on switch, not something which time will yield. That's why it's important to get started now. You don't want to wait another year, another decade, half a lifetime before beginning. Everyone knows the result: a buildup of unexamined emotion, which, if it lies untended, grows elephantine even as it buries itself inside you. Again we see the usefulness of memoir, a kind of prophylactic against forgetting.

TO WHAT DEGREE IS *A.H.W.O.S.G.* a portrait, as Sarah Lyall suggested, of the author celebrating "a pure joy in living with his younger brother, to whom he acted as parent, companion and frequent partner in mischief"? To what degree is the book a portrait of an author who obscures, perhaps necessarily so, the pain of his own adolescence by dwelling on the "pure joy" of today? Eggers sings and responds, antiphonally. He celebrates and obscures, at times within a chapter, a section, a paragraph. And yet this sidewinder motion is also moving him inexorably toward facing his past.

As much as Eggers tries, pulled about by his hedonistic buddies, he can't put back in the bottle what the MTV interview has uncorked. The top blown, the run ends. Hands up, exaggerator! We're the truth squad, and your irreverence is under arrest. From page 239 on Eggers knows, semiconsciously it seems, where he and book are going: an even more intense display of a) the glib self-expression he and his friends fashion with the magazine and b) the effervescing loss of his parents. In the penultimate chapter, Eggers returns to Chicago to make some sense of their deaths. There's work to do. Locate the ashes. Reconnect with an old girlfriend. Endure the bitter wind off Lake Michigan. Entering again, like blasts of arctic air, are his father's tyranny and his mother's complaisance. Why are they so strong? Simple. The force of re-membering them can no longer be shaped and scuttled by irony. Surprise! He thought he was hugging the shore, but he's floated out to sea. Where there was no undertow, there is one now—and it keeps pulling.

Anguish and desperation overtake the sense of the ending. There are passages in Eggers's last chapters where his imagina-tively exaggerated fear (which is nonetheless real) gets the better of him. Why, he rattles on and on, doesn't he take Mom's cre-mains to the Atlantic Ocean? Much more fitting. Why dump them in "ridiculous, small, tacky" Lake Michigan (207)? Eggers is getting a bit daffy, perhaps, narrating the recent past and *its* most recent present—neighboring suddennesses. He "mis-remembers" his mother's funeral, recalling it one way, only to be corrected by those who were there and remember it, we presume, as it was. Passages are devoted to "I don't know if what I'm doing is . . ." (take your pick) wise, right, meaningful, stupid, disgraceful. His memories of his parents and his childhood are so troubling that he loses his footing. Now, then, tomorrow, next week alter and flow together. Time out. Eggers hastens back to California to deal with a peevishly suicidal friend, John. He's driving John to, and paying for, a private rehab program. The argument they have on the way contains the following turnabout. John speaks first.

> "Sorry dude. Sorry I bore you."
>
> "You do. All this unbelievable whining, uncertainty, the wallowing—"
>
> "Please. Look who's talking. You're one to talk about dwelling on this shit, your family shit. You're the one who—"
>
> "We're not talking about me."

"Yes we are, of course we are. We always are. In one way or another, we always are. Isn't that obvious?" (423)

In the last section, which is unlike any other in the book, Eggers juxtaposes several times and voices in slapdash succession: while he and Toph play Frisbee, memories of his mother and a sort of self- or reader-aimed anger intercede. It's very Zen, and quite disturbing. Frisbee; Mother dying; Frisbee; anger; Mother; Frisbee; cancer; why doesn't this all make sense? The energy of this passage must be read to be grasped, so hysterical and defensive and corrosive and (even) out of character it is. A fiendish tongue inhabits the final pages, a pure id, crocodilian. Present and past have wholly interpenetrated. The coitus has produced a sort of child-beast, venomously spitting in its own face.

HOW UTTERLY ASLEEP I WAS during my six-year marriage. How utterly stunned I was when it ended. I could no more have written about that experience right after it ended than—But why? Why do I say that? Because I didn't write it about then? Because my journal, whose self-coddling, self-pitying forays, that year, 1982, proves I couldn't feel it? Because I had few precedents (like Eggers) to show me what memoir could do? Because the antiseptic mode of autobiography prevailed in the culture, saying you need time to pass, you'll only get sucked back into the dreck if you write about it now?

This fearlessness is what I admire about Eggers. *He gets sucked back into the past as he writes about it.* That's the point. He learns he can't free himself from the past, so he must supply the physical immediacy of what he's just gone through/is going through. His personhood grows by oscillating back and forth between doing and being, between "no crying in memoir" and giving in to introspection. Sudden memoir is about being insecure, remaining insecure for the extra innings of insight. The strength of this approach is also its weakness. To be closer to recent experience, the sudden memoirist writes and formulates quickly. Engaged, the writer may become hostage to such a review. Writers have ritually penned their daily grind into daybooks, journals, diaries, from which scenes and descriptions for later (much later) attempts at fiction or autobiography emerge.

But Eggers's way is not diaristic. He has none of the "jotting it down as it happens" quality that inhabits Catherine Texier's *Breakup: The End of a Love Story* (1998). That book records nine months of in-time fury at her husband's betrayal, a man whom she cannot let go of even as he stays (and sleeps) with her and beds his mistress three times a week. Texier is brave in telling how her sexual/emotional possessiveness keeps her chained to a man who doesn't love her anymore, with bad effects all around. But the book bogs down because of its obsessive recycling of Texier's jealous anger. Not doubt this was how she felt as the molten rage leaked or streamed out. But the portrayal of a dominating emotion, however accurate, feels vengeful and shortsighted. Memoir is not put to good use. Texier lacks the self-in-the-world quality that Eggers has, refocusing the drama onto things relational (Berkeley, family history, graphic design, fun, little brother) that could have enlivened the pace of her book. There's plenty of action (screaming, crying, lovemaking), but her character is not moved, that is, changed by the action of the story. Her memoir can't satisfy us, since there's so little emotional growth. Which may be what all memoirs (even the sudden ones) need: variously growing and sufficiently moving emotional progress.

9

What Is Telling the Truth?

Some Kind of Liar

I wish I had taken a friend's warning about memoir and family;
it's engraved in my mind (now) like an eleventh commandment:
"It's more important to whom you *don't* show your work than to
whom you do." My mother was one of those "don't show"'s. I
mailed her a long story about an incident in our family's early life
that had always troubled me. She was on the phone one week
later, chastising me for putting us in a snowstorm the night Dad
drove her, my two brothers, and me away from his parents' home
in Evanston, Illinois, following a fight my father had had with
them. "I don't remember any snowstorm, Tom," she said. "That's
all in your imagination." She sounded absolutely sure. I remember—I *think* I remember—the snow that night: hard, wet, Hitch-
cockian flakes. I remember my father's leather-gloved hands clench-
ing the wheel, his temper coiled inside him. Too bad he wasn't

alive, after I began writing about our family, to confirm the snow one way or the other.

Mother disapproved of my stating in the story that she and my father undervalued Dad's parents' home. "They didn't have room to put us up," she said, "not because my folks offered, as you suggest, a better Christmas, but because his folks had only two bedrooms." But her parents *did* offer more. They were wealthier. Their Victorian home and elm-darkened yard on State Street in Rockford, Illinois, was many times the size of an Evanston walkup. For me, from ages three to fifteen, that equaled a much finer Christmas, the Frank Capra holiday we all cherished.

In short, Mother didn't trust me with spilling the family's beans. What parent does? Most interrupt the child's telling, convinced there's a correct version that the progeny must be told to remember. Mother sensed, instead, that as a writer I was up to something. (Or, to put it in a less accusatory way, it was my "imagination" that corrupted me, made me artistic when others, like her, suffered or indulged no such streak.) The snowstorm made her suspicious, and my preferring one grandparent's home to the other cinched it. If I could falsify the weather, she reasoned, wasn't I likely to overstate or make up other details, too? Besides, where did I get this "ability" to recollect word-for-word dialogue, describe the exact wrapping-paper colors of the presents under the tree? It didn't come from her, she said. Then, unprompted, she added, "The past is over. Nobody cares about all that anymore." *All that* for me was the alluring inexactness of memory, made palpable and profound via my first forays into writing memoir. But Mother felt such exposure would soil our name. For me to write about anything of our past would be to remove it from the family memory, which carries unalterable certainty, and place it into the public record, which carries unnecessary shame.

"You're not going to publish this, are you?"

I didn't tell her I already had. In fact, I never told her, for she died about a year later.

In retrospect I think she may have been most confounded by what she perceived as a literary writer's concealment. She used to say that in college (Northwestern, class of 1941) when her English professor asked the students to ponder a poem's meaning, she'd recoil. Meaning made her blanch. She wasn't smart like the others, she said. She could neither find nor articulate any nonobvious interpretation in Robert Frost's "The Road Not Taken," for example. She wanted to be told what it meant, not endure the treasure hunt. Meaning emerged with discussion, but that didn't defuse her view of authors: They were, by nature, mystifying what could otherwise be clearly stated. For her, an imaginative author was some kind of liar.

Several years before this incident, I had begun writing about my father. When I told her, she thought that my endeavor would be a chronicle of his life—adopted at birth, Depression childhood, college, Navy, war, paper-seller, marketing director, retirement one month, death the next. In her mind there was no difference between the life he lived and the life I would write. But I was recalling the *character* of my father in my eye, the man whose intimacy (which she didn't know he and I shared) was central to my growing up. Once she discovered I had made Dad a character, she thought that I was designing a work to be different from what had been, that I was artistically (or criminally, or devilishly) pursuing something more grandiose than honest. Something else, but what? Dramatic exaggeration? Embellished truth? Parental favoritism? The father-son prerogative?

When she questioned me, my defense was, I'm writing memoir, not practicing chicanery. I tried explaining that memoir recalls the past from an author's subjective view. But it does no good to tell that to a nonwriter, particularly a relative who figures in your work. (I did ask her what she recalled, some of which I included in subsequent pieces. But memoir is not an exercise in family togetherness. What I wanted to tell was my memory's story in addition to the so-called actual one. I still can't say what I was hoping for when I sent her my piece: that her approval would allay my guilt at having written about us?) I wish my mother could have known how much I struggled with what was appropriate to reveal, the times I've censored myself in favor of others' feelings, the times memory and I have overacted those feelings, the times I've wondered what exactly the truth was about the past, knowing (now) that my snowstorms were her flurries.

As it turns out, I'm glad I showed my work to my mother. Had I not, I would never have known how stridently families differ about the past. I would not have seen, as Mary Karr did in her book, that families manifest typically the most primal and potentially the most duplicitous relational experiences we have. It struck me how important it was to be labeled a fabricator by one who was not an editor, a colleague, a friend, any of whom might have accused me of glorifying a formative scene from childhood and had no problem with it. Such rationalizing went nowhere with my mother. She was the adult; I was the child. She was responsible for what had happened to me; she had created and overseen (with my father) the world I grew up in. What she remembered needed to be heard.

Her sensitivities did not alter what I wrote. They did convince me, however, that memoir affects others in ways I hadn't realized. If I was to continue writing memoir, I had to learn why nonmemoirists often accuse those who do indulge in the form of inventing some of their material and why the accusation is loathsome to any writer who is interested in telling the truth. Isn't "telling the truth" something we'd all agree is important to us as individuals? Yes, obviously. But in memoir what *is* telling the truth? And whose truth are we telling? These are among the form's thorniest questions; perhaps one way to find some answers is by contrasting memoir and fiction.

The Blurry and the Blurred Past

In the roman à clef, a form of the novel also known as autobiographical fiction, the novelist changes names and dates, disguises places and descriptions, creates composites out of characters whom the writer has known. The novelist may also make herself a composite. And yet she leaves in enough of the known so that characters are identifiable *and* masked (roman à clef is a "novel with a key" that opens the door to the actual). Kathryn Harrison explored her incestuous relationship with her father as fiction in *Thicker than Water* (1991) and as memoir in *The Kiss* (1997). Each book had its purpose: the first, to dramatize the experience at a distance (maybe to feel it less as *hers*), the second, to activate the emotional veracity of what happened *to* the author (though, ironically, that book also feels distant but less so). One critic, who approved of the novel more than the memoir, deemed the first "literature" and the second "psychotherapy." Harrison said that she wanted to get beyond victimhood because she was "no longer satisfied by working through the material in terms of fiction" (Hulbert).

Thanks to Harrison and other authors of the last twenty years, memoir is getting more comfortable with its niche beside fiction and within the sphere of narrative. Though Harrison's two forays were grounded in the author's choice, each has a unique purpose: a novel emphasizes the emotional truth of a character while a memoir emphasizes the emotional truth of the author. That both forms are also dramatic, descriptive, characterizing—all things narrative—does not change their purpose. The question is, what is important about emotional truth *for the author* that must be disguised or altered? If I write about my sons as a memoirist, I could change their names, birth dates, friends, and so forth. But, once I started changing their traits, what would be the point? If I were no longer involved in the actual emotion of our relationship or if I were to feel constraints that would invade their privacy, I would relinquish the memoir mantle and make fiction. Again, both forms yield self-discovery, either through the novel's character and for the memoir's self, whether it's the "I" of Huck Finn or of Thomas Larson. And yet even with the fictionalized autobiographical "I," this authorial dimension for the novelist has not been as deep, as risky, as intimate, as shape-shifting as it has been for the memoirist. (Read Mark Twain's autobiography for a sense of how Samuel Clemens fought with *his* "I," and then read Huck Finn for a sense of how Clemens celebrates Huck's "I.")

Fiction is not designed to push you toward the personal truths of your life. Fiction was *never* designed for that. Fiction equals persona, which suggests theater, which implies epic, which involves myth—all of which, as in the case of Huck Finn, gather the tribe as community. To be nonpersonal and symbolic and alive with collective meaning—those are the foundations of make-believe. Our understanding of fiction's rhetorical purpose doesn't sharpen memoir's rhetorical purpose. It's no wonder that some memoirists aren't clear about their own veracity, the uneasy place of tension between fact and memory that writing memoir has thrust them into.

We've all seen the prefatory statement that anchors many memoirs. Such declarations are ahead-of-the-gate testaments, usually penned after the book is finished, to clarify the author's intent. Here's Deborah Digges, from *Fugitive Spring: Coming of Age in the '50s and '60s* (1991): "In the process of completing this manuscript, I've heard many voices besides my own, correcting and editing. I've taken liberties when it came to recreating dialogue and setting. Now and then I've collapsed time, invented details. If there are mistakes, they're mine. *Fugitive Spring* is a version of a story. I wanted to write it while we are, most of us, alive." The author's admission may sound appropriate, but I'm not sure for *what* or *why*. Will her misremembrances hurt her family? Are her fabrications intentional? Whatever she's trying to clarify she seems to remuddy. How are we to know, for example, whether Digges has made mistakes? Her best friend's blue eyes could have been brown (which she changed as a way not to identify that friend among others). But readers would never have known. To say there may be mistakes is to say there *are* mistakes. Moreover, such an admission seems aimed at her characters who are, no doubt, some of her readers (as my mother was mine). Would it be possible, if a mistake did occur and Digges wanted to set it right, that maybe in an afterword (in a later edition) she could alert us and make amends?

Molly Peacock prefaces her *Paradise: Piece by Piece* (1998) with this:

> In beginning to write this book, I wanted to tell the story of the decision how I chose not to have children and found myself telling a story of my life as a poet, teacher, and as a sister, daughter, lover, friend, and wife. This led me to face two necessities: Seeing the truth as I saw it and protecting other people's lives. The central family players—my parents and sister, grandparents, cousin and my husband, Mike—are all real. The other characters and some events are invented or transformed. *Paradise: Piece by Piece* is a hybrid memoir both true and truer in the sense that fiction trues ideas against the blurred realities of life.

Peacock says that she has hybridized her memoir by marshaling fiction's ability to "true" ideas, which nonfiction cannot do. But narrative nonfiction "trues" ideas via story all the time. Read Jon Krakauer or Gay Talese. What is Peacock's intention: to accrue virtue for cleverly using fiction or for conceitedly making memoir? My question is, why not engage life's "blurred realities"? Why must we use fiction to "true" or balance them? Are realities blurred by a writer's need to imagine and inject a false event? (Perhaps reason is what's blurred.) Or does the past arrive at memory's door already out of focus? If the latter is true, then is clarifying the blur an act of fiction or an act of memoir?

You'll see these quizzical prefatory statements a lot more in the coming years, in part as a reaction to James Frey's *A Million Little Pieces,* to which a lawsuit-savvy preface has been added after Frey's lies were exposed. These prefatory testaments feel like contrition, tinged with misgivings about the "act" of memoir. I think any author must hold himself accountable for his memoir. And where else should he do this but *in the writing.* It seems so obvious. But still, few memoirists understand how co-creative accountability and remembrance can be. Many pre-Frey writers (since no one complained) have had it both ways.

Erica Jong, author of *Fear of Fifty* (1994), has said, "I've always thought that the idea of genre was a blot on the soul of literature. Categories like novel, memoir, biography have no value when you're writing—however much value they have to librarians or bookstores. A book is a book is a book. I suspect that the idea of genre has silenced more writers than it has liberated." She cites Henry Miller, who "didn't care about genre. He thought fiction and autobiography were one and the same. He predicted, in fact, that in the future the lines between genres would disappear—as they have—and he refused to recognize distinctions he thought were stupid" (201). The categories have no value? Jong and Miller, as much as I admire them, are dead wrong. In *The Catcher in the Rye,* J. D. Salinger needed fiction to serve the concentrated drama of Holden Caufield's psychotic episode over three crazy-making days. Even if he "were" Holden, it is the moody desperation of an introvert that Salinger gets right, not the unlikely genre-mixing truth that only he would know. Were it memoir, the reverse would have been true.

There's another problem—I don't trust the libertine Jong. Fabulists and other genre-benders, by definition, don't possess the regard for personal truth that memoirists do. I think Jong wants to bully memoir into joining the fiction writers' team. In her zeal to dissolve boundaries, to buddy memoir up to fiction, she thinks creativity will be compromised. And yet to distinguish the memoir as its own is why writers have developed the form. We deprive memoir of its singular character if we lump it into fiction simply because we know that any personal narrative has irremediable fictional traits. In recent years literary novelists have become adept genetic engineers, ingeniously interbreeding history and fiction. Michael Cunningham's superb *The Hours* (1998) interlocks its fictional tale with the "facts" as written in Virginia Woolf's *Mrs. Dalloway* (1925). No one I've read has a problem with such borrowing. Nor is anyone claiming that fiction, because it uses facts, should be a subset of history because facts are essential to both. Thus, it doesn't make much sense to say that memoir is fiction because memoir uses elements of a writer's imagination. The savvy memoirist presses on, despite the fingers-crossed prefaces to some otherwise very good books. We must resist being fiction's handmaiden and develop memoir's creativity and autonomy to make it a form unto itself.

One more thing. You can accuse a fiction writer, as in the roman à clef, with using actual people and experiences as subject matter, but so what? No violation of autobiographical truthfulness has occurred because fiction exists as fabrication. You can accuse a memoirist of writing fiction, but that's not comparable to what the fiction writer does. Fiction's falsification is entirely different from that of a memoirist. The whole point for the memoirist is to resist falsification and, at the same time, be aware that narrative embellishment can take any writer over the edge.

I prefer the "in your face" memoirists: those who tell the story of some aspect of their lives along with—and as significant as—the force that remembering the life and searching for its meaning has played in writing the story. One of the most brilliant postmodern memoirs is Geoff Dyer's *Out of Sheer Rage: Wrestling with D. H. Lawrence* (1997). The book's subject—Dyer's wish to write a critical study about the work and life of Lawrence—is replaced by its doppelganger, a diatribe about the difficulty of writing a book about the work and life of Lawrence, which is spun out and becomes a book about that difficulty as well as the work and life of Lawrence. The book he didn't intend to write *is* the book he ends up writing. In it, you'll see Dyer straddle confession and criticism, undress his own putative authority, and thereby, enlarge the possibilities of memoir.

Rambling Our Lies (after Andrew Hudgins)

Despite my drawing a line between memoir and fiction, the messiness of fact and memory in memoir remains. How do we know whether we're being truthful to the facts, of others' lives and of our own? Can our honesty overshadow our stories? Memoirists evaluate their work as judge and jury, witness and prosecutor, freethinker and moral authority. A few of us are actually burdened by these roles. In a daring essay (originally titled "An Autobiographer's Lies" when it first appeared in *American Scholar*), Andrew Hudgins, a Southern Baptist and a poet, takes himself to task for embellishing his poetry. In a memoiristic essay, he owns up to what he's fabricated and why, cataloging eight lies, "in ascending order of transgression from misdemeanor to felony" (93).

1) the white lie, or leaving stuff out;
2) the "lie of narrative cogency," or adding details;

3) the "lie of fictional convention," or self-mythologizing to make oneself more literary;
4) the "lie of emotional evasion," or not writing about the things one is truly ashamed of;
5) the "lie of the re-created self," or making oneself look good by emphasizing the right events that will bring out the writer's better behavior;
6) the lie of "extended consciousness," which involves (a) appropriating other people's experiences as our own and (b) applying adult experiences to the child's experiences and making it sound as though the child experienced it;
7) the "lie of interpretation," or emphasizing a narrative arc of one's life so that one's life has a meaning and significance it may not have had;
8) the "lie of impressionism," or remembering events and people with such exaggerated feeling that what is written has little to do with how what actually happened affected the people present: this lie is done on behalf of emotional truth and is "inescapable for a writer attempting to create an artistically coherent work." (92–106)

This may sound too facile and after-the-fact. But listen to Hudgins, poet and penitent, as he testifies to wrestling with these lies, not by revising every poem he's written, but by deepening his sensibility to, and developing a standard for, the truth in his work.

Grudgingly, I went back to work, trying to make sense out of material—my life!—that I had resisted making sense out of because first I'd have to understand it, and that understanding could be tentative, provisional, and painful. Then I'd have to forgive it, which is painful. Then I'd have to ask for forgiveness, which is even more painful. Then

I'd have to write it all down through many drafts, which means going through the whole ordeal over and over again. Aesthetics and psychology are uncomfortably interwoven, but in autobiography the warp and woof is pulled even tighter than in most fiction because the writer's own emotional, spiritual, and intellectual progress becomes the aesthetic progress of the book. (102–3)

There's a motto for the discerning memoirist: *In autobiography the warp and woof are pulled even tighter than in most fiction because the writer's own emotional, spiritual, and intellectual progress becomes the aesthetic progress of the book.* We reach a sublime summit, where memoir's usefulness is its aesthetic. Hudgins concludes with a surprising pronouncement: despite being guilty of "lying" in some of his verse, the four books of poetry his deceptions have wrought have all been worth it.

Quickly, back to my mother. Where in Hudgins's compendium would she have put my snow-white lie? Numbers 2 and 3: adding detail and self-mythologizing. Maybe a tad of number 5: making myself and my dad look good by making the situation appear worse than it was. While these are low on Hudgins's scale, my mother would have judged my sin of commission far worse than Hudgins would have. For her, it was personal. It was an affront to her adult witness, to her belief in an ineradicable past, and to the memory of the man she had married, who had died and who was now being cast into print by (me) the only person who (there's no doubt this is so) would have ever bothered to cast him at all. For my mother, it wasn't about gradations of deceit. It was about my not honoring her memory and my father's memory, an old-school notion that hopes for a "fitting memorial," a ritualized, public, safe way to be remembered.

If Hudgins's list of the memoirist's transgressions is valid, and writers see the hierarchy differently than how others have witnessed the same events, what can we conclude? The memoir writer faces ethical responsibilities he's unaware of. Anything he remembers will be disputed. At the same time, he has to find a way to keep the quarrels in his corner. The reason we write memoir is not to dispute the past with others but to discover how the past is disputed within us. And yet I also think we have an obligation to bring the competitiveness of memory within a family, if that's the field, to the surface. This is another of memoir's callings: to stir the pot of recollected experience enough so whoever was there sees, as the writer must, that no single version will suffice.

Hudgins's hierarchy asks us to hold ourselves to a standard that says how we remember, why we remember, and how our remembering affects our families and friends *matters*. Saying it's "like" fiction, or saying it's okay to fictionalize events or make character composites as long as you center on the underlying truth or message, is both a cop-out and irresponsible. The truth—not the fiction and not the imagination—matters if you're going to write memoir. But let's be clear about the truth. Truth is factual and emotional. The former must never be falsified. Indeed, the more we adhere to what's accurate, the more we get to the other side of the equation, the emotional truth. Emotions, unlike facts, are well armored against our glibness as storytellers. Not only do we fear the chaos of emotion, but there are protective, ritual-bound, secretive feelings others hold for us, many of which we carry, that may keep us from writing the truth about ourselves. To put these competing emotions, within us and among intimates, into motion in a memoir gives it part of its story.

10

Which Life Am I Supposed to Live?

Getting This One Right

By now I hope it's clear that the memoirist is she who sticks with the form long enough to undergo changes in how she sees the past. The act of memoir writing and its river of recollections has made her different from the person she would have been had she not traversed the rapids. The act has also changed and deepened those predictably indulged and semitrue stories she's been telling herself and others, no doubt, for years. This is one reason my mother took umbrage at my messing with the family's past, which she felt she had greater ownership of than I had. She wanted the past left unexcavated. Such digging, she rightly intuited, would change *her,* forget about me. Honest reevaluation guarantees revising what was. It may also include the unintended: discovering why my life turned out far different from what it could have been.

At age thirty, I was a composer and a musician, on track in music school toward my PhD. But then, in 1983, my wife yielded to her anger at me (maybe at herself) and ended our marriage in a matter of weeks. The change was so devastating (I was broke and homeless for a time) that I reevaluated my musical path, which I believed I had freely chosen. Alone, and writing again, I saw that composing and playing music was a cover I used to keep myself from what I really wanted to do, write. (I had begun writing in high school and college but left it behind in my early twenties to seek a career as a performer, then a composer.) The music covered things up in two ways. First, I poured myself into scoring musical ideas and practicing the guitar and the piano, which removed the self-reflective quality of writing. And second, my love of playing and composing had me awestruck: this was what I was meant to do. That daily *played* embrace of the guitar—held on my lap, tucked against my chest, wrapped in my arms, fingertipped to life—lured me like the Sirens. Until one morning, as I was waking up in my van in a suburban neighborhood, it dawned on me that one art (music) might be keeping me from practicing another (writing). In other words, my affinity for music was deceiving me, had turned me, in a sense, against myself. How strange that the world of tone and rhythm could take me away from myself, though at the time I felt *away* was my home.

All this taught me about music's deviousness. From lullaby to dirge, music expressed my emotions, ruled out my self-analysis. Memoir writing, which I took up postdivorce, expressed *and* made sense of how music and literature had divided me and become my identity. Telling the story of my artistic affinities and delusions told me that there is a small yet fierce Armageddon between our divided selves, the person I think is me and the person who is me.

I want to explain this self-split in simple terms first. The *author*, who is writing now, tells a story about the *person*, who has lived and is the subject of the work. And yet it's never that easy, for author and person are intimately bound up. I, a memoirist, was once, not that long ago, a musician. I relate to him then as an author now. As I write—narrative action, summary, dialogue, statement, telling details, inner monologue, to characterize that other—his individuality grows, at times, beyond my control. The person I was can easily become as important as he once was to me.

Ah me, the abiding one, the one who unites our past and present selves, and transcends them. That abiding me I like to call the *core*. In my case, I was duped by a sense of myself, the composer-musician, as the person I hoped to be. My musicality led me away from my core. But music also took me through my core, for there was something quite appealing about being a musician that was also *me*. I was duped, but I was willingly duped. That person was the lost artist of my youth, a fully integral part of myself who had to be lost before he could be found. To be a musician was *not* to express my core self, despite its somehow being integral to that core.

What a quandary. To what degree have I been on a mythic journey? To what degree have I blazed my own trail? To what degree have the roles of family, culture, generation, race, ethnicity, gender entrapped me? To what degree have I revolted against these expectations and found myself? The consequence of not attending to the core is stated in the Gospel according to Thomas. "If you bring forth what is within you, what you bring forth will save you. If you do not bring forth what is within you, what you do not bring forth will destroy you" (Pagels, 53). Despite the quote's mystery, I think that what's churning within us must be brought forth so we might be saved (perhaps redirected) from what is a truly personal evil—the wasting of ourselves by ignoring our individuation.

In *The Woman Warrior: Memoirs of a Girlhood among Ghosts* (1976), Maxine Hong Kingston rejects the female traditions of Chinese culture, the imperative to be loyal and deferential, even though these things are a strong part of her identity. In feminist revolt, she goes against what she has internalized, even made her own. But that does not mean she merely throws off the daughter's duty like an old coat. To revolt against such duties is to revolt against herself. The amount of distress this causes her, as well as the mix of guilt and liberation she feels, attest to the pain of disinterring her core self, whatever that is. Carl Jung named the internal quality which our civilization and traditions collectively suppress, and is always alive and forming within us, the "undiscovered self." And it is the story of this *truer* self that we discover and disclose in memoir.

Nuala O'Faolain's Somebody

One intriguing tale many contemporary memoirists tell comes from an author who makes the discovery—as he writes—that his life has had meaning once he contrasts the life he expected or wished he had lived against the life he actually has lived. Leonard Kriegel, who has written both memoir and critical articles about the form, expresses this dynamic well. Having contracted polio at age eleven and been confined to a wheelchair ever since, he knows better than most the life he might have had. He writes, "For the obsession with the self in its places matched against the alternative self in its unfulfilled moments remains both the fulfillment of autobiographical writing and the greatest danger facing the autobiographical writer." Many writers are forced "to relive the past that is never quite the past one wanted." The person I never became haunts me and raises the bottomless query: how can the reality of what didn't happen be as strong as the reality of what did? "Between who one is and whom one might have wanted to be," Kriegel notes, "can also be the source of the writer's deepest, most useful, tensions, a maelstrom of turbulent and uncharted waters" (210).

Kriegel's dilemma is this: If what I'm living now is not the life I intended, then a) what *was* the life I intended, or others intended for me, and I didn't get to have? and b) how does that unlived life inform the one I ended up living? Such questions electrify the memoirist's fingers—I am not what I intended myself to be, so therefore the choices I have made were made for me by some alien within. There are a couple of psychological ways of regarding this visitor. One is the hero complex. *Had I married Terri, had I stayed in New Mexico.* Those roads would have led me to my true career, to love, to happiness. There I might have seized the destiny I have today but with fewer blows. But this is a conceit that wilts under reason. *Had I married Terri, her desire that I convert to her religion would have meant (I know now) separation and divorce. Had I stayed in New Mexico, I would have never gotten the writing opportunities San Diego offered.* The other perspective, a contrasting view, is that these might-have-been's bring stability. A self we could always return to, a self we should keep striving for, a self we can never be—all pump up the pontoon that keeps us afloat. They are necessary supports for our egos, which carry a kind of survivor self that rationalizes what is, especially if what is has gone bad.

An unlived or escaped fate is central to Nuala O'Faolain's *Are You Somebody? The Accidental Memoir of a Dublin Woman* (1996). O'Faolain is often surprised that she didn't end up as her mother did—alcoholic and married to a man she adored and despised for "giving" her nine kids. To them her mother offered little of her affection, which she saved for reading. Following a bookish path in her own adulthood, O'Faolain earned a PhD at Oxford, taught at the University of Hull, worked in London as a television producer for the BBC, traveled widely, and finally returned to Dublin to write, as her father had, a column for the *Irish Times.* "My mother was as unaware [about her choices] as I was," she writes. "'I don't really care if you get a degree or not,' she wrote to me, 'I'd far rather see you with a husband and a few kids.' This—even when her burning resentment showed that she felt as trapped as a slave, kept out in a suburb with children!" In her mother's time, the cultural mandate—"that it was desirable for all women to go

off for their lifetime with one man and have his children" (82)—
went unchallenged. O'Faolain fled the other way: she had a series
of affairs, many loveless, though one, with a woman for fifteen
years, was quite enriching.

Throughout the memoir O'Faolain cannot escape the shadow
identity that she felt she should have had—to be as unfulfilled as
her mother. It was close: had Nuala been born one generation
prior to women's liberation, she would have been doomed to her
mother's fate. And yet the very release from her mother's prison
brought an unknown she was equally unprepared for. To avoid
the shadow identity of her mother, O'Faolain moves on from
everyone. In the final chapter, which one critic describes as "one
of the most perfectly observed portraits of female loneliness" ever
written (Heller), the childless and relationless O'Faolain spends
Christmas Day by herself, ruminating about fate and choice. Place
memories fill her mind. Their power permeates the memoir's ele-
giac ending. She tells herself that she should have come across a
meaning by now. She must be cursed because the golden thread
that will tie her choices together hasn't arrived or (worse) doesn't
exist. All the events and the people she has known, she concludes,
are "discrete": "near each other, and made from the same material,
but never flowing into each other. That's how the life I have described here has been. There has been no steady accumulation; it
has all been in moments" (188). Which, surprise, may be what her
mother once felt as well.

The U.S. edition contains an afterword in which O'Faolain
describes the popularity her book enjoyed with readers in Ireland.
A familiar face from television, she's often asked, on the street,
"Are you somebody?" It's not celebrity that O'Faolain treasures.
Rather, it's that she tapped into the wishes of thousands of Irish
women, the nobodies who've wanted to be somebody, the daughters who've wanted to be different from their mothers. *Oh, to be
somebody*—the life I should have had. A life still wrapped up in

Mother's approval. On the book's last page, she wonders whether all the places she has been and described "are for me what books were for my mother? They are altogether full of promise. They assuage some of the regret for all the lives I never had" (188).

Among the paths she regrets *not having* and which some of her readers regret having taken themselves is the one her mother wanted for her—to be consumed by a husband and children. And yet Nuala regrets many of her own choices, involving married men, staying in and leaving Ireland, staying in and leaving England. Had she followed one or the other of these choices, would she by now have had experiences she would have *not* regretted? The ambivalence is thick. How strange to regret what you never had. Had you lived another life, one you didn't live, wouldn't it, too, have been filled with regret? What exactly do we regret—the having or the not having? Still, to be guided by what might have been, as masochistic as it may sound, is valuable to the memoirist. Even though your life went the way it *did* go, its meaning stems not from how it went but how it went awry, against or despite the way it should have gone. I am the person I am, who is also the person I didn't imagine myself becoming. Central to my self-definition is who I thought I'd be and my wondering why I didn't become him. He whom I wanted to be and didn't become, I am.

The memoir we end up writing, like the life we end up living, is what O'Faolain calls "accidental." Purpose for her is mediated by two paths she forsook: her mother's way and her imagined way. Reexamining the accidental may be our story, a neurotic part-song of not-quites and what-ifs. Down among the what-ifs lies the core. O'Faolain knows that she would have ended up like her mother had she not said *No.* But saying *No* to her mother and to others carried her into the temple of loneliness where our mothers dwell. O'Faolain's mother was lonely for her daughter's life, which she desired and couldn't have, just as her daughter aches for her mother's life, which she didn't desire and wouldn't have. Nuala's despair may not contain the objects of her mother's resentments. But it swarms with resentment, nonetheless.

Ambivalence Engaged

In his essay "The Past Breaks Out," Alfred Kazin sharpens the paradox of self-identity that many memoirists face, Nuala O'Faolain among them. Kazin's *A Walker in the City* (1951) is a beautiful evocation of his sensuous childhood and adolescence in Brooklyn in the 1920s and 1930s. He writes, nearly four decades after his memoir appeared, that "a key to my book is of course this constant sense of division, even of flagrant contradiction between wanting the enclosure of home *and* the open city, both moral certainty and intellectual independence. This conflict has never ended for me, I confess, which may be one reason why, thirty-six years ago in Pineapple Street, I felt I was at last discovering an inescapable truth about myself and no doubt other Jews of my generation brought up on the old immigrant poverty and orthodoxy. To rebel against the tradition was somehow to hold fast to it" (Zinsser, 133–34).

The push-pull of "moral certainty and intellectual independence" is Kazin's nexus. He didn't know that, while young, he'd been steeped in a contradiction: to value Jewish Brooklyn, a Jew had to leave it. This insight may have never wholly occurred to Kazin until after, perhaps much after, the act of memoir. Such was the conclusion of Marguerite Duras, too, who said that for her writing is "a matter of deciphering something already there, something you've already done in the sleep of your life, in its organic rumination, unbeknownst to you" (25). Similarly, my musical past no longer feels "prior" but rather forever gnaws at my heels. My love of irregular rhythms, of textured voices, of crafted dissonance (à la Charles Ives) all shape the prose I try and compose: my musical sensibility saturates my writerly one.

In *A Walker in the City,* Kazin moves from the quiet pre-dictability of Brooklyn to the stentorian chaos of Manhattan. At the close of the story, he enters college, launched on his path. (As we know, he will become his generation's best literary critic.) It would seem that youth—he is a keen noticer and preserver of Brooklyn's old-world community, Brownsville—has brought about his success. Too pat, I fear, for the memoirist. To write about one's life is to work out one's identity, never encased in amber. Willa Cather once said that "a creative writer can do his best only with what lies within the range and character of his deepest sympathies" (851). Those sympathies are stacked in the DNA; they are the nature of our character. (Character here refers to the quality of the self's interests and desires.) Thus, character or quality of self is as much there when it begins to develop as it is there when it shows itself during its development. But Cather and Kazin, you and I, must do our best with what we're given. Which is to say, we must grow into who we are, never knowing exactly what it is we are growing into (though memoir offers the chance to find out). Thus, we must see Kazin give texture to the sounds and smells of his mother's cooking, to the mischievous activity on his block, so we can feel his physical love of home while his self-liberating identity drives him away.

To possess this drama, the memoirist's self must appear to us as it develops, even as it is jostled to and fro by its nature. Kazin's self can't simply be ambivalent and conflicted. The conflict has to engage his ambivalence. How do we know his core is developing? He lives it, then names it. The more he rebels, the more he realizes his rebellion defines his Jewishness, insofar as that identity is inborn and ongoing. How do we know O'Faolain's core is developing? She lives it, then names it. The more she distances herself from her mother, the more she shares the loneliness her mother feels.

A memoir of my artistic life intertwines my musical and writerly sympathies. Their joining and unjoining is the uniqueness of my character. Though I may have become a writer at the expense of leaving a musical career behind, I can never excise the musical aspect of my creativity. Nor would I. My discovery is the straining pull between these sensibilities in me; their sinewy attachment is my story.

LET ME EXPLAIN THIS IDEA about the ambivalence we discover about ourselves in memoir another way, via the progressing story of one writer I have worked with in a memoir group.

Vicky is writing about her most influential teacher, a nun named Sister Mary John, who fascinated Vicky and her best friend during fourth grade. The year was 1969, and Sister Mary John was young herself at twenty-two. She was strict like other nuns in their Catholic grade school. But she was also, as Vicky recalls, "creative, dedicated, and intelligent." She had them read poetry and put on plays in class. She also made herself available to the nine-year-old Vicky with an ardor that showed itself in special treatment and meaningful cards. Vicky said the feeling was not sexual but thick with intent: *you should not be confined by rules; you should make something of yourself.* (Advice, it turned out, the nun was ruminating on herself.) The influence was felt in the moment: Vicky saved everything from that school year. A few grades later, after Vicky herself had been kicked out of the Catholic school, she heard that Sister Mary John had left the convent (she'd lasted ten years) but not teaching: she had earned a PhD in education. Vicky also heard that Sister Mary John had been charged with violating her vows as a nun by growing "too attached to some of her students," Vicky among them. "It was a nun thing—not that she had acted inappropriately; if she had been a public school teacher," no one would have cared. Years passed, Vicky grew, but her emotional connection to Sister Mary John remained. One day, she and her friend decided to find her. They discovered that the woman had retaken her original name, Adele, that she had married and divorced, and that she was now a psychologist and an author. Recently, thirty years after fourth grade, Vicky found Adele. The first thing Adele told her was that she had kept a photograph of Vicky and her friend (as well as other favorite students) on her wall—all these years.

One night, Vicky's story is the topic of group discussion. "So why," someone asks, "was she so attracted to you?"

"I don't know why," Vicky says.

"Since you've made contact, why don't you ask her?"

To find out why would be easy. Hearing Adele's explanation, Vicky could add that element in, dramatize it as part of her story. Group members encourage her. I wonder how Adele's recalling why she singled Vicky and her friend out will inform Vicky's story. How much can we apply the insight of others into our character *as* our character? Is this a kind of foray into biography, letting others have perspective on our experience?

A month later, following a series of e-mails between Vicky and Adele, she tells us that the former nun got so "attached" to her because she felt a "underlying sadness" in Vicky with which she, Adele, identified. The sadness concerned her and she reached out. That sadness was also what Adele felt for herself—sadness about her difficulty with remaining a nun. Vicky identifies the emotion more specifically as "an 'old soul depth' in me." She feels this is what her former teacher felt. Vicky says that her soulful bent "was due to the pressure I felt from my Catholic indoctrination in believing that I had to live my life like a saint or like Jesus— and knowing that, I would never be able to live up to the standard. I also worried about the concepts of Heaven, Hell, Purgatory, and Eternity. These thoughts kept me up at night. I think I just wanted to be loved for who I was and not for being the saint I could never be."

This sadness or soul-worry has permeated much of Vicky's life. She recalls how it shaped her home life: the last of seven kids, with a distant doctor father and a busy mother, she had a youth much less parentally intimate than she wanted. And yet behind her acting out, her rebellion, the soul-worry reigned. It felt to her that she spent much of her youth (and some of her adulthood) avoiding it. Such a core trait may have been recognized only by a person like Sister Mary John, whose heart was similarly turned. This is compelling. It suggests that our stories may be unlocked, even activated, by others who know our shadow selves better than we do. Of course, these others must be accessible and interrogatory if they are to be useful.

I find it surprising that someone else would have a say in our identification of self. It opens up another relational line for memoir writers. Perhaps we need to search our own sensibility as well as to tap the perspective of others for formative experiences that initiated our character into the world. For Vicky it may have been a watershed not only to have her emotion validated by Adele but also to have Adele name it.

Now that Vicky has a theme to explore, she needs to write. Fourth grade and its players must be recreated from her vantage now. She must show us Sister Mary John singling her out, seeding and cultivating her rebellion with those cards and her attentiveness. She must show us a scene in which the nun acknowledges Vicky's sadness, perhaps a scene during a play or a poetry reading that dramatizes how it might have happened, making it clear that she is imagining. She must show us other scenes, too—about her home life, about the good/bad influence of other girls, and about her specialness in school (outside of home) that may have been launched at that time. After conferring with Adele, she may even want to dramatize how Sister Mary John separated from the Church as well. There's a thematic link between characters: Vicky and Sister Mary John rebelled against the strictures of Catholic school. What kind of life were they destined to live (recalling Nuala O'Faolain) had they not escaped? Vicky and her teacher, each in her own way, triggered the other to defy those expectations. And, maybe most important, the drama of Vicky's sadness, as it remains in her still, is revealed as the wellspring of her memories.

Vicky is haunted by Sister Mary John's approval and the nun's ability to see inside her. The reason, she tells me, lies in the lasting hold such a once-habited, now-free woman has had upon her. Vicky is drawn to and repelled by many things, not just the Church, she says. My comment is that during fourth grade Sister Mary John activated the kernel of Vicky's character *in* Vicky, insisting that she, like Sister Mary John herself, was drawn to and repelled by all sorts of things, one of which was her own sadness. We might call this kernel *ambivalence.* Examining her relationships with her former teacher, her family, and the wider world for ambivalence may clarify Vicky's feelings about who she is today and whether that person is the one who will write the memoir.

11

Memoir and the Inauthentic

The Persona and the Self

Willa Cather's nugget bears repeating: "A creative writer can do his best only with what lies within the range and character of his deepest sympathies." Her aphorism suggests that because our sympathies as writers are several, so, too, are our narratives. And we can't do our best if we stray from these sympathetic narratives. Can you hear the enigma? The one fact that may unite us all, author or not, is that we *have* strayed. Straying is our story. We are writing either to return to or to rediscover our core values, say, a passion for dogs or the Battle of Gettysburg. The "range" of the lives we've led—less often directed at and more often wandering from our "sympathies"—*is* the lives we've led. Aren't we all characterized by that which we did not achieve and never got? Don't all memoirists discover that in looking back there is as much pain associated with failure and dead ends as there is curiosity in finding our condition different than what we thought it would be? One thing Nuala O'Faolain learned is that she turned out okay despite being primed by the course her mother hoped she'd follow. The person O'Faolain became is now called *not her mother's desire.*

But such a gain—to be somebody who recognizes her sympathetic self—takes time. Many memoirists have a ways to go, in living and in writing. Getting there, each of us must confront the nobody-ness of our pasts, where the less-than-traumatic truths dwell, if we are to know ourselves. As memoir writers now, we have to see what we see: that being less evolved and still whole is logical madness. "Life," John Lennon said, "is what happens to you while you're busy making other plans." It's tough to think of the vagabondage and accidentalness of our lives as our authentic paths. Rather, we're apt to think that the off-ramps experience and fate have led us onto are *inauthentic,* that is, in conflict with what we imagine or hope or know our core selves to be.

WHAT A WORD TO DROP in the memoirist's lap! Inauthenticity. Eventually I will discuss its partner, authenticity, a word equally loaded. But the idea I'm developing here is that memoirists, in the process of writing about conflicts between self now and self then, discover that they are bedeviled by the inauthentic. The reason I want to write about the past is that the past houses a person who is not me, a faux me, a me who relinquished some intrinsic authenticity to become *I.* The best way to unpack the inauthentic is to first examine the term *persona.*

We know from literature that writers adopt a mask to tell a story. Novelists and dramatic poets, descendants of Homer, often talk about how important the mask, or the adopted voice, is to telling a story. This mask or persona is used to project a character, who is not the author, into the world with a tale that may spring from the author's sensibility. J. Alfred Prufrock is the mask T. S. Eliot places upon a character who is, we assume, not Eliot, so that

Eliot can express his own fear of personal change via Prufrock's confession, "I shall wear the bottoms of my trousers rolled." If an author uses actual people from life, say himself and his family— D. H. Lawrence called *Sons and Lovers* an autobiographical novel about the Lawrences—the writer may still fictionalize facts and alter traits for artistic reasons. The devotion Lawrence felt for his mother was more explicit in the novel than he may have expressed to her in life. Shakespearean drama posits the as-yet unchallenged persona of a king or a prince, whose veil is lifted by way of familial deception, even murder, to expose the complex, unknown, authentic person underneath who suffers the unmasking.[1]

One reason we are curious about the fashion model, the newscaster, the celebrity is that such a glossy surface must have some skeletal support: no one can be that shallow or pious. Politicians baffle us because we, far more than the politician, believe the mask he wears hides the unscrupulous. The way a public person acts obscures the genuine. But the word "genuine" (like "authentic") is also loaded. Americans loved Ronald Reagan because they believed that his affable persona was no act, it was the real deal. The persona, however, so controlled the man that he was fully comfortable *playing* Reagan, a man who, according to Edmund Morris, lacked thoughtfulness and was emotionally cold to his children. (The likely truth about positions of power is that they draw narcissists who are very good at camouflaging their personal desires from themselves and their constituents.) No one can get elected in America unless he or she wears the disguise: religious, prayerful, not in therapy, a party loyalist, a patriot, straight, security-minded, and so on. And yet, once in office, few are ever as one-dimensional as the role demands: the stresses of the job make them human, which is to say, they slip into behaviors common to the rest of us. After all, one needs private values in order to have them corrupted. In contrast to Reagan's pure persona—he was the same in public and in private—Richard Nixon's authentic self was fully present in the conversations taped in the Oval Office, where we heard a master-builder construct his self-delusions. Take this psychopathology a step further: think of the hand-wringing betrayal we unleash in ourselves once we unveil the very people we have demanded wear the mask.

The word "persona" has a specialized definition, which I take from Carl Jung: the outward manifestation of certain parts of our personality. This is the person we are in public, the person our culture or society wants us to be. It is also the mythic sense we have of ourselves as writers, parents, citizens, even moral beings. To the world we present a professional or predictable or mythic self. We assume that if certain parts of our personality are projected outward, there is room for an inner person who is more complex and controls the projection. And yet, as we've seen with Nixon and Reagan, the man behind the curtain may or may not exist. It's obvious that our inner self must be squelched by our roles. It's less obvious that the squelching has actually stimulated the inner person to evolve (perhaps to write memoir or go into therapy) because the contemporary persona demands so much. Jung, who believed the persona to have expanded dangerously during the 1950s (the last decade of his life), calls this bifurcation of role and self a "painfully familiar" division that creates "two figures" who are "often preposterously different" (94).

Let's apply Jungian terms to the life-writing distinctions I made earlier. Autobiography is written by the public person who tells the birth-to-death story of her persona. By contrast, the memoir allows the authentic self to lift the mask and tell the story of how mask and self have been intertwined. (What a shock to find there's so much inauthentic *to* tell.) The memoir's aim is to beget the authentic self to come forward, to assume the mantle: expose the inauthentic. For example, Dave Eggers lights out from the territory of his parents' deaths, only to discover, in the end, that he has to embrace the grief he's denying in order to be less lost. Memoirists become the person who unmasks the persona; the unmasking is a liberating act. The opportunity to free oneself from the iniquities and delusions of inauthenticity may be memoir's greatest attraction.

We lie to the world as a matter of course. But understanding the lies we tell ourselves, which support our lies to the world, is a vastly different project. Such lies undergird the myths we live by, the myths that compel us to write memoir, and the mythic new individuality memoir writing can produce. In *I Know Why the Caged Bird Sings* (1970), the eight-year-old Maya Angelou is raped. To grapple with the trauma, she quits speaking. The book is, in part, a record of her not speaking, which becomes her mask. But in writing down the keenness of her silence, she becomes who she was: a literate voice, the real Maya, who has not died. By the end, she is talking in and to the world again, but now as witness. The book stands, literally, as her vocalized recovery. Such memoirs trade in the mythic unmasking and mythic remaking of the self. The process for the memoirist is to dig into her personae and inauthenticity, where the lies and myths are seeded and grow, so that she can tell the story of how those lies and myths have buried her sympathies and core self.

From Inauthentic to Authentic

We're all intrigued by our strangeness in the world and to ourselves. And yet we also think that beneath the bug-eyed sphere of fate or role or profession, there—*there!*—our core selves reside. It may follow then that if I feel my core self has been lost or mislaid, I can use the memoir form to locate that person, the writer who through self-examination might know himself, at least in the latest incarnation.

I love this aspect of memoir as self-locator. But we must be careful not to overplay it. Memoir can only arouse the writer to go in search of the self. "In search of" is key. The self, certainly no object to be fenced and flagged like an acre of land, is a process or current that flows toward and away from itself. Once we realize that the here and now has the greatest control over the personal narrative, we are saying, in effect, that the core self can never be found. It can only be activated now and in the succession of now's memoir writing activates.

With Virginia Woolf, we see her voicing in her diary, journal, letter, sketch, the value of her authentic self. Her subject is often her creative core. (Except when she was depressed, she seldom seemed beset by inauthenticity.) In *Context Is Everything: The Nature of Memory*, Susan Engel writes this about Woolf. "It is hard not to come to the conclusion that she lived her life, at least in part, in order to write about it" (116). Woolf "experienced daily life with an autobiographical stance: How will I say this? What does it mean? How do I feel? Is this significant? One imagines that these are the kind of questions (conscious or unconscious) that rant through her mind while in conversation, working in the garden, walking, running errands, or in other ways living the life about which she would write" (117). It is intriguing to wonder whether Woolf's enthrallment with questions about memoir and mortality may have surfaced via the limitations of writing itself. That her suicide was caused by the German bombing, which in turn fueled her depression, is probably true. But there's also a tragic incompleteness to her life suggested by her suicide: Had she glimpsed the therapeutic potential of memoir writing and had this discovery come about too late to save her?

Contrast Woolf's brief and momentous "Sketch" with a memoir by another writer stylistically very different: F. Scott Fitzgerald. (Woolf and Fitzgerald died within four months of each other: she, a suicide, in March 1941, and he, a heart-attack victim, in December 1940.) Like Woolf, Fitzgerald also wrote a late-in-life sketch, briefer than hers but just as gripping. His confession took apart his deepest wound, his own falseness. "The Crack-Up" originally appeared as a three-part essay in *Esquire,* between February and April 1936. In an introduction to *The Jazz Age,* a collection of Fitzgerald's memoir essays, E. L. Doctorow writes that Fitzgerald's regret contains a surprise. The man did not leave *himself* out of his musings. Instead, the pieces reveal that Fitzgerald was, in Doctorow's words, "haunted by his inauthenticity—as the young Lieutenant in his World War I overseas cap who never got overseas, as well as the urbane young Author carried on the shoulders of his generation, [quoting Fitzgerald] 'who knew less of New York than any reporter of six months standing, and less of its society than any hall-room boy in a Ritz stag line'" (ix).

The novelist Fitzgerald used the personae of Dick Diver, Nick Carraway, and others to reveal how the greediest generation saw the worst among their kind. It was one reason why Fitzgerald was lionized: he nailed the Roaring Twenties. But reading those novels we had no idea the extent to which their author yearned for personal authenticity. Gin-soaked, he wrote a brilliant, caustic fiction that he says papered over a personal life that had grown (with and without Zelda) shallow and unreflective.

Such is the theme of "The Crack-Up." (Fitzgerald's "sketch" of his mental break predates Woolf's "sketch" of her mixture of memories by three years: alas, both writers only dangled toes in the sea of self-revelation.) Saying that he had "landed" in Hollywood as a rewrite man in 1935 (he first came out in 1927 to write screenplays), Fitzgerald realizes that "I had weaned myself from all the things I used to love—that every act of life from the morning tooth-brush to the friend at dinner had become an effort." Even literature had taken a fall: "I saw that the novel, which at my maturity was the strongest and supplest medium for conveying thought and emotion from one human being to another, was becoming subordinated to a mechanical and communal art that, whether in the hands of Hollywood merchants or Russian idealists, was capable of reflecting only the tritest thought, the most obvious emotion" (66). He had done "very little thinking" (67). He had lived superficially. He had far less conscience than most of his contemporaries. He had no political stake. And—his reason for confessing—he was being brought back to life and conscience by men, he says, who were much finer than he was.

But then Fitzgerald realizes what his inauthenticity, his inattention to an inner self, has birthed. It's a new being, clumsy and naive, one barely sheathed by an ego. He says, "There was not an 'I' any more—not a basis on which I could organize my self-respect—save my limitless capacity for toil that it seemed I possessed no more. It was strange to have no self—to be like a little boy left alone in a big house, who knew that now he could do anything he wanted to do, but found that there was nothing that he wanted to do" (68). Whereas Woolf celebrates the tissuey link between memory and self, Fitzgerald is dismayed at his emptiness. And yet there's a glimmer of identity, based, undeservedly, on his self-denunciation. In the psychologically similar rise and fall of their lives, Woolf and Fitzgerald both sought refuge (dare I say healing) via essays in nonfiction. They seemed to be piloting part of their creative impulses toward a new memoir-enabled self just before death took them by surprise.

IT WOULD SEEM that like our personae, our inauthenticities would be public expressions, easily seen through. But they aren't. They're a mix of seen and unseen. Fitzgerald rues his faked life, which he says he was seldom conscious of as he lived it, particularly in the 1920s. Nor were his friends; indeed, they were likely codependent, seldom straight with him, the exception being his late-in-life intimate, Sheilah Graham. Likewise, Mary McCarthy had to befriend herself in order to wake up. In *Memories of a Catholic Girlhood* (1957), she collects her published remembrances (mostly magazine pieces from 1946 to 1955) and, as postludes to each, confesses what was and wasn't true in the originals. The interchapters, in which she owns up to her inventive memory, are enthralling. They ring with authenticity and raise concerns about her poetic license. Ever the gimlet critic, McCarthy seems to have initially performed her childhood in prose and later felt obligated to review her performance. That reviewing self arises from the primal, sympathetic Mary McCarthy, who had been lacquered over by her literary and leftist persona and was unleashed by her conscience.

Was McCarthy that unaware, as she wrote those pieces, that memory would mislead her? Had she been overtly lying to herself? It's tough to tell. Lying implies intent, and intent, we all know from the defense attorney, is difficult to prove. We may know what happened; we may also choose to lie or say we don't know or don't remember. I think, after reading her self-flagellation, it's more accurate to say maturity fertilized her memory. In the original stories, a number of factors led her to write as she did. First, she says that since she and her brother were orphans, they have a "burning interest in our past, which we try to reconstruct together, like two amateur archaeologists" (6). Clearly, some of the conjecture was wrongly reported. She cites her father, who "was a romancer." "Most of my memories of him are colored, I fear, by an untruthfulness that I must have caught from him, like one of the colds that ran round the family" (11). She blames her fiction-writing facility for coercing her to arrange events in the quilted patterns of a good story: "Many a time, in the course of doing these memoirs, I have wished that I *were* writing fiction" (3). But, when she finds facts she misstated or interpretations she remains ambivalent about, she calls herself on the carpet for her "lack of self-awareness" (8). She follows by disputing the "dubious points" (47) one by one. A typical example: "I was discovered coming into the gymnasium after meeting a boy one spring evening, shortly before graduation. I think it was Miss Gowrie who caught me, but I am not positive. Sometimes I feel it was and sometimes I feel it wasn't" (165).

It is the duo-drama of presenting these points as story and then as shadowy exaggeration or outright lie that earns McCarthy the award Best Author in a Supporting Role. Even for a misremember, round two recall is formidable. Her intent becomes her theme. (Would the same self-scrutiny have happened to McCarthy's bestselling nemesis, Lillian Hellman—whose three memoirs from the 1950s and 1960s are, as McCarthy famously charged, riddled with lies—we might have been less prone to second-guess as many memoirs as we do now.)

Most memoirists have neither the notoriety nor the self-scrutiny that McCarthy did and that publishers and public intellectuals sought from her. If anything, the contemporary memoirist would integrate past event and his attitude toward it in memory now as *one* story. Some of us have written a version of a personal turnabout, but then have revised it substantially because the writing itself had changed us. Along the way we've seen the power of continually turning back to memoir, even the same memoir, as the means of uncovering more about ourselves. We turn to memoir to regain our lost or negated characters and sympathies. We turn to memoir to question and judge past decisions in light of how those decisions have played out over time. We turn to memoir to finally see our ambivalence, our somnambulance, our mistakenness, our deceit, our most egregious fibs.

All this *turning to* by the memoirist turns around the capstan of the authentic self. Unlike the sum-happy autobiography or the sin-absolving confession, memoir allows a reanimation of, and a relational bout with, one's authenticity. Memoirists feel this is a fundamental goal of their work: to take the time it requires to reclaim that self. In reclaiming the self, the memoirist becomes the person the writer would like to be, a writer-hero, perhaps, who is more authentic today than the person she is remembering. One of the certain beauties of McCarthy's *Memories* is an honesty about herself that she finally reached in her life. This moral stance toward self and literature (I think of Lionel and Diana Trilling) was once common among American critics.

An honest narrator is an authentic narrator, one we can root for. We root for Sylvia Fraser to free herself from the psychic prison of sexual molestation, and she uses the memoir form to that end. We root for Primo Levi in his several Auschwitz-infused remembrances—the best is *Survival in Auschwitz* (1947)—to be among the handful of Jews the invading Russians find, skeletal but alive, in the camp. We go to these memoirs knowing their authors have made it out, even in pieces. Which suggests that we want more from them than a survivor's tale. But what? Transformation? Wisdom? We want the writer to explore and inhabit the tension between the authentic and the inauthentic; we want the memoirist to see himself stirring the heroic and the ordinary together. Here there's ample friction, when the self-congratulatory dimension is as great as the self-authenticating one.

12

Two Selves Authenticated

Rick Bragg

Who better to root for among the likeable protagonists of recent memoir than Rick Bragg, the hero of *All Over but the Shoutin'* (1997). Bragg is the lovable southerner, the bootstrap poor boy of the 1970s. His tale has two parts: his Alabama childhood, during which he is raised by his unselfish "Momma," and his journalism career, in which he rises to the top. He's got two lofty desires. First, he wants to repay his mother for the sacrifices she made while raising him and his two brothers; he is determined that she have her own home, which he'll buy as soon as he saves the money. Second, he will earn the down payment by being the best journalist he can be, eventually joining the staff of the *New York Times,* and winning recognition and awards. This is not just a storybook life, but one he's already made happen in accord with his plan. Life makes book—one of the ways it's supposed to be with memoir.

Bragg casts his journalist's vocation as one of hardship, in which he parlayed a chip on his shoulder into reportorial success. From where comes his anger? His alcoholic father (a ruined Vietnam vet) has abandoned the family, in essence sentencing them to poverty. Bragg and his brothers are raised by their mother, who does field work, cleans houses, and takes in laundry and ironing. She is nothing short of a saint: "She walked around with her toes sticking out, but we got new shoes" (75). What's more, Bragg acknowledges the guilt he feels for having watched his mother wear the destitution on her sleeve. She went out "only to buy groceries." "It was a long time before I realized that she stayed home because she was afraid we might be ashamed of her, ashamed of the woman with rough hands like a man and donated clothes that a well-off lady might recognize as something she threw away" (74).

Since Bragg has never had it easy, he gravitates to trouble. He relates a number of fast-driving and girl-crazy stunts that, as an adolescent, almost land him in jail. As a reporter, he volunteers for or is sent on the most arduous assignments. He writes of other people's pain in flinty and affecting prose. Though he covers riots, civil war, murder, and tornadoes in the South and the Caribbean, he never shares these with his mother on his frequent phone calls. Rather, he lies to her so as to assuage her worry: life's tough enough as it is. Still, his mother's plight is always on his mind. His debt to her drives him psychologically and materially. To buy her a house, he must succeed in the moneyed world. The small-town gazette sportswriter makes it to the *St. Petersburg Times* and their Miami bureau; then, after a stint at Harvard in a journalism program, he's hired by the *New York Times*. His page one stories win him a Pulitzer Prize, the money arrives, and he buys Momma the house.

Behind Bragg's success is gnawing unease at what his family has endured—his mother's piecework and his older brother's jobs, among them loading coal and castrating hogs. Bragg bows to their labor. Although he does some backbreaking jobs while young, he realizes that he will in time "pass" this kind of work; his writing talent and his tenaciousness to see his talent through will take him far. But as he rises, he tells us his brother is shackled to "a long, long walk, where the scenery seldom changed." The point is, writing will never compare to those jobs his family must hold: their trials "would make every other job, every other thing I ever did for the rest of my life, so laughingly easy by comparison" (103). The hyperbole, the poor-me tone, is thick throughout: Bragg refuses to affirm the intrinsic value of his own work. Writing and farm labor are not comparable, but he persists in elevating one over the other.

Such commentary muddies things up: if Bragg so honors his family's labor, then why does he focus less on their difficulties and more on the self-aggrandizing world of his writing? The "shoutin'" is more about him than them, less about him *through* them. Besides, it rings hollow to say that you value what others have done far more than what you've done, but then to show that "every other thing [you] ever did for the rest of [your] life" *did* have value, in large part, because of its financial and personal rewards. And yet Bragg insists on skewering himself: "I picked one responsibility [being a reporter], just one, and I met it. But, any fool can meet just one responsibility. Any lame idiot can set the bar so low, and clear it" (318). Winning a Pulitzer Prize is setting "the bar so low"?

Though he tries to downplay it, Bragg's book is really about *Bragg's* success. Since that success means everything to the son who left, it must mean everything to his mother, too. If not, he will make it mean everything. When Bragg makes good on the gift of the house, it comes with fresh family turmoil—Bragg's younger and older brothers get into a fistfight in front of the house, causing the mother to move back (temporarily) to the place she had lived in and hated for thirty-five years. Bragg has what amounts to a fleeting realization about his authentic self. "I knew," he writes, "that maybe I had bought this house more to redo the past than to make her dreams come true" (323).

What happens to Bragg and his family materially is a fact. What happens to Bragg emotionally—to his authentic self—he leaves dangling like a chad on a disputed Florida ballot. The war that Bragg says is within him never flares. He says that he fails at all interpersonal relationships, but he never shows us a scene in which he fails. If there's any fight in him, it surfaces vicariously in the lives of his mother and his two brothers (one is responsible, the other goes to prison). Or the fight is set up as an false dichotomy: Harvard (where he receives a fellowship) and the *New York Times* as the elite and false world are bad while high school football in Alabama and eating cracklin' are good. This split alone suggests Bragg's inability to see complexity outside his experience—that there might be good people at Harvard and stupid people in Alabama who are good or bad not by virtue of where they live or where they were educated but by virtue of who they are, individually, morally.

Thus, Bragg doesn't seem to grow in the memoir—with the memoir: he's seldom interested in examining the effect of his family's victimization upon him. He does admit to dishonesty: "I hear it said a lot, especially lately, what a good man I turned out to be, considering. I always feel like a poser when I hear that, because I know it's not true." Rather than seeing his own "meanness" as a flaw, he writes that he "channeled it. I used it every time I told some loving soul that I had to say good-bye because my work was more important to me than them, or just because it was time to move on." Bragg may say that he knows he's plagued by his hard-charging reporter's life, in which he's forever running out of time. But, in the next breath, he's on another airplane, hell-bent on doing his job and saving for that house. The result of such single-mindedness is, "I have no home, no children, no desire for them" (318). And that's it: a man full of "meanness" who doesn't appear mean or broken at all. If he's beleaguered by any of this, it doesn't show. He's content to state his confusion and let the mix of home-loving southerner who can't go home again *be* him. He plumbs the persona, not the self on whom the persona rests. Not only does an authentic self not exist for Bragg, but by the end of the book he doesn't know it doesn't exist.

A memoir writer becomes a memoirist when he evolves through the dramatic and analytic presentation of his perspective. He writes with and against the persona, or, at least, writes aware of its power. I'm critical of Bragg because as he digs for news, he seldom digs for *his* news. The passage Bragg says he's gone through—up from the downtrodden yet pulled back by his roots—is a ritual act that regional cultures demand of their brethren. It's a familiar two-step: faithfulness to home, to the goodness of everyday folk, to hard work, to doing for others. All these things Bragg feels he's failed at while he's succeeded at (and disparages) the choices he's made. What's denied—and, in Bragg's case, it's also fully desired— in self enrichment. It feels almost like a sin for Bragg to want what he wants. It's this bird-dog loyalty that victimizes him. I'm not arguing that the belief is misguided. I am arguing that *All Over but the Shoutin'* is a missed opportunity for Bragg to see for himself just how trapped by the "should"'s of southern culture he is.

Some memoirists like Bragg purchase their self-image from the regional storehouse. I am my history. I am what my people have suffered. I am "my people." Which begs a question. Do my class and heritage, region and schooling, make me who I am? Bragg concludes that yes: his public self is his private self. Perhaps in this impersonal realm there is an individual truth for many readers; resisting that private self may be the only means by which traditional values are upheld.

Elizabeth Wurtzel

As Bragg fills out his southern persona, readers hope to identify with him. He did it, he told his story, he made an impact. Why can't I? But watch what happens when a writer heads against the grain. Away from self-justification and toward self-revelation. Away from the found self and toward the lost one. There are memoirs—more plentiful than Bragg's—in which the author is dead set on parading her ugliness, a self readers have trouble rooting for, in part because it's obvious the girl needs *help*. In fact, we would like it a lot if she were to (please) curb some of the confession and puff up a bit more persona so that we might root for her.

One such narrator is Elizabeth Wurtzel. Her *Prozac Nation: Young and Depressed in America* face-slapped our staid notions about life-writing when it appeared in 1994 and continues to wreak havoc and change lives, typically for the twenty-somethings. Wurtzel's confession describes an illness in search of a diagnosis. In fact, the book *is* the diagnosis because it lays bare what's wrong. Wurtzel is severely depressed and the illness drives her unmercifully: to boyfriends with whom she confuses sex and love; to relationships without boundaries between her and her friends; to regular public spectacles of her emotional meltdowns; to drugs like Ecstasy, Valium, and Percodan; to self-analysis (her memoir-nature, manifesting at a young age, tests our patience); to rage at her divorced parents; to alcoholism while working as a young reporter; to stalking men; to psychotherapy and psychoanalysis; to antidepressant and antipsychotic drugs; to a diagnosis ("atypical depression"); to a suicide attempt (an overdose of Mellaril) of which she writes that it "startled even me" (315); and, at last, to salvation in a pill, Prozac. And all this before she's twenty! "In my case," she writes, "I was not frightened in the least bit at the thought that I might live because I was certain, quite certain, that I was already dead. That's the thing I want to make clear about depression: It's got nothing to do with life. In the course of life, there is sadness and pain and sorrow, all of which, in their right time and season, are normal—unpleasant, but normal. Depression is in an altogether different zone" (22).

Wurtzel's depression begins when she starts cutting herself with a nail file as an eleven-year-old; the depression runs its course in a climactic suicide attempt from which she is rescued, at twenty-one, by her female psychiatrist, Dr. Sterling. Along the way, we are lacerated by her ups and downs; on many of the 368 pages we are faced with some emotional outburst about her disease. For example, there's

Blame: her parents were "constantly at odds with each other" and gave her an "empty foundation that split down the middle of my empty, anguished self" (29);

Self-pity: "all this . . . is no more outstanding than the plot of an Ann Beattie novel. Or maybe it's not even that interesting" (33);

Regret: "All Timothy was to me that night was all anyone ever was to me at that point: a new person to sob to" (197);

Confusion: the typefaces alternate without reason between italic and roman, perhaps to dramatize her shifting moods and manias;

Stupidity: "I am so desperate to believe that I will like it there [London] that I completely ignore the fact that I hate Blake and Dickens and all those other writers, that I switched from majoring in English to Comparative Literature because I pretty much hate the whole British canon" (263);

The infrequent bit of wisdom: "A human being can survive almost anything, as long as she sees the end in sight. But depression is so insidious, and it compounds daily, that it's impossible to ever see the end. The fog is like a cage without a key" (191);

And, finally, gratitude: of Dr. Sterling at McLean Hospital Wurtzel writes, "It is only because of her determination and dedication that I survived that year without actually being committed, and it is only because of her that I am alive today at all" (237).

One of the many targets of Wurtzel's frustration is her mother, who is strangely in sync with her daughter's foundering. Mom is helpless and angry; she's passive-aggressive; and she's a nurturing enabler, who wallows in the family's divorce. And yet, how can we blame her? Elizabeth is her daughter, a hater, a victim, and a chronicler of her mother's codependency. Wurtzel says her Pollyanna mother "wanted to keep things as good as they could be" between them (53). This is long after the divorce (her parents split up when Wurtzel was two, but continue to fight until the father, fed up, abandons her and his support). To the lost mother, daughter becomes buddy and in this guise is named Ellie. Ellie is the pliant girl; she is Mom's "date" when necessary. After school and on weekends, she "hangs out" with Mom because Mom needs a friend. But there's a cost: the author cannot completely run away and go wild as she hopes to. Why? "Because my mother would not be able to survive such a personal debacle" (53). Her mother is dependent on her daughter's staying partially grounded, which means that Wurtzel can never—around her—feel as bad as she feels. "You should be telling this stuff to Dr. Isaac [Wurtzel's childhood shrink], she'd say every time I tried to talk to her about my depression. It's not that she was insensitive—sometimes she actually would try to talk to me about why I was like I was—but she just couldn't stand it when I'd explain that nothing at all was wrong, that it was just a matter of everything" (53–54).

In a poignant scene, while Wurtzel listens to Bruce Springsteen's "The Promise," crying uncontrollably, her mother begins screaming at her and demanding to be told what's wrong. Wurtzel can't say: she doesn't know what's wrong. Later in the story, her mother does what she can to keep Elizabeth in therapy and on antidepressants (which also take a toll). But the travail between them has a kind of ab ovo helplessness about it. Not only are they incapable of helping each other (forget about living up to their mutually exclusive expectations), but they are also co-codependents. "After a while, it was always like this: I'd be lying helpless in my room, she'd be lying helpless in hers, there was nothing we could do to make each other feel better, and the whole apartment seemed stuck in some miserable detente" (54).

The number of such helpless incidents is many, each time ignited by Wurtzel's acting out. All hands, even the psychiatrists', are blistered by her drama. And yet to watch her entwine shock and understanding is to be transfixed by her plight. Her unmasking of herself in memoir is far more digestible than it would have been in real life, had she been *your* friend or *my* daughter.

I FIND *Prozac Nation* captivating because Wurtzel is such a cogent self-pesterer. The book clearly inflicts her suffering upon us. But it also records the inflicted pain upon her, almost like the shaman who enters a trance or a trial by fire to remind others that her crack into the other world is still open. The book astonishes us for how much of her persona the author takes on, leaving us with some big questions. To what degree can an illness *be* a persona? To what degree is her depression *her?* To what degree does her acting out help her survive the lousy hand her genetic dealer has dealt her? If her core self is a depressive, what self does she use to counter it? Her persona?

Let's back up. Wurtzel's now-narrator sees into the persona-self divide as she recalls her self-mutilation at eleven. She remembers hiding from everybody, typically during lunch period. She feels completely alone: different, fat, incorrigible, unloved. "Every so often, I would sit in the locker room on the floor, leaning against the concrete wall while my tape recorder sat on the bench, and I would fantasize about going back to the person I had always been" (45). Who's that girl? One who likes to play tennis, who's well adjusted and unafraid of school, kids, teachers, and her parents. She's the girl Wurtzel feels inside, a girl she can will herself to be, especially if her tendency to act out goes overboard.

A tendency to act out what? The wishes of the "dead person" she feels herself becoming, the person she believes is her "alternative persona" (45). Indeed, Wurtzel thinks (wrongly, it will turn out) that her good *inside* girl is "adopting" this persona, calling it forth. Who's this girl? She is a death-obsessed eleven-year-old with a cache of antiauthoritarian talismans that include Patti Smith records and Swiss Army knives. Wurtzel thinks that this insurgent will defend her—the inner "authentic" child—against her fears of being unloved, against her need to be outrageous. She reports that this persona is "a put-on, a way of getting attention, a way of being different. And maybe when I first started walking around talking about plastic and death, maybe then it was an experiment. But after a while, the alternative me really just was me. Those days that I tried to be the little girl I was supposed to be drained me. I went home at night and cried for hours because so many people in my life expecting me to be a certain way was too much pressure" (45). This tearful girl is overpowered by the actual person inside Wurtzel, that is, her core self, a depressive. The tearful girl, the fighter, will try to get rid of what she believes is an alien persona. But the alien is actually the depressive self overtaking her.

Wurtzel's discoveries, from the chapter "Secret Life," dramatize the onset of her illness, and they are among the most remarkable in the book. "I remember being in a panic one day at school," she writes, "when I realized that I could not even fake being the old Lizzy anymore. I had, indeed, metamorphosed into this nihilistic, unhappy girl. Just like Gregor Samsa waking up to find he'd become a six-foot-long roach, only in my case, I had invented the monster and now it was overtaking me. This was what I'd come to. This was what I'd be for the rest of my life" (46). What is occurring to her has already occurred: *I had, indeed, metamorphosed.* She's already been cursed with the depression gene. And yet she thinks that she's inventing this trait as she gropes through adolescence. Her self-invention (no wonder some severely depressed people become artists) is really the illness talking. A teen can't know that depression switches on one day. A teen has scant reflective ability. But a teen feels responsible, and she carries this idea that she's responsible until she becomes trapped in its pattern.

It's all topsy turvy. Elizabeth Wurtzel's core self is her depressive core, even though to readers it seems that the disease must be a persona, an outward expression that keeps her from being her true self. We so want her not to be ill that we've decided Wurtzel's inner Ellie—if she and we want it bad enough—will save her. Thus, the story goes: Ellie the Good gets projected onto Wurtzel by mom, dad, friends, boyfriends, colleagues, teachers, who hope she'll stop being depressed and start being herself. The tension builds because friends and family believe this crazy girl is not Ellie. So, too, does Wurtzel. She buys the diagnosis. Throughout adolescence. The tragedy is that not only does such an inner savior not exist, but its nonexistence is revealed time and again by everything the depressive girl touches. Why does it take so long for Wurtzel, family, and even a few therapists to see that her core is depressed? It's culturally counterintuitive to think that the internal Elizabeth is a self-mutilator, a teenage drug addict and alcoholic, a stalker, a narcissist. It upsets our fantasy of the innocent adolescent who would never desire self-destruction. In fact, *Prozac*

Nation proves that the more we think her core pristine and her acting out merely a false part of her personality, the deeper and wilder her illness grows. We think that the core self can't be sick. But the core self can be incorrigibly hostile to the person's survival.

In short, our notion that people need to draw on their inner resources to get better doesn't work for depressives. (It doesn't work for cultures and classes of poverty, either, but that's another book.) Depressives *can't* get better; they can only—we're learning—get therapy and medication. Such anodynes may help them adjust. But that may merely be going against what we want them to do— adjust to us, to what's "normal." The lesson is, we have to adapt to them. What's more, in a culture too slow to reform its attitude toward depression, the depressive must adapt to herself. Kudos to Wurtzel. She lived prior to the "wellness" movement and somehow got through. One mechanism for psychological wellness is, of course, Prozac. And yet we think of Prozac as an artificial drug that does the work of personal health all of us should be able to do. But Prozac is merely an agent that helps the depressive be like us, that is, not or far less depressed.

Winners versus Whiners

Why put Bragg and Wurtzel side by side? I realize the contrast is extreme: Bragg has none of her illness and Wurtzel has none of his South. Bragg's arrival seems clear: he's at peace with himself, he and his persona are one, he's gone as deep as he cares to go and the depth he's gone couples heritage to self, which is his point. In fact, Bragg would be putting on airs if he were to say that he is any more than the wayward son of a hardworking and self-sacrificing Alabama mother. Wurtzel, on the other hand, counters the folk hero. For one, she doesn't have a persona or a self in which she can take comfort. For another, to be who she is—a core depressive— is the last thing she wants. Because of the nature of her illness, she can't really claim a self whom she has seen herself become. In fact, if she is to have a self, it can begin its stint only when the book ends.

Bragg wins accolades as a reporter and does right by his Momma while Wurtzel overdoses on pills and stalks her boyfriends. The self Bragg projects into the world as a memoirist is beloved, in part, for what he's done *for* his mother. The self Wurtzel projects is nothing close to beloved, in part, for what she did *to* her mother and *to* herself. As others have cheered, I, too, felt the big-heartedness that Bragg bestowed on mother and state. And, like others, I, too, often wanted to strangle Wurtzel.

On the Do-You-Love-Me scale, readers root for Bragg to make it—how we adore winners—while readers feel Wurtzel, the Drama Queen, is incapable of "making" anything—how we despise whiners. Winners versus whiners. Both authors appear to have written memoir to show that each did the extraordinary, has been transformed by events, ended up better off than where either began. Both *are* better off, though it's a lot harder to say what Wurtzel achieved. Nothing like Bragg's honors.

Memoir drags behind it (to paraphrase a poem by Robert Bly) the long bag of the self-made man—he/she is modeled for us in autobiographies of celebrities and CEOs, in countless great-man feature-length screen bios, in rock star videographies where the singer's fall from drug addiction is countered by recovery and a new CD. Model precedes making. When the self earns the tangible, its path is validated. What Bragg wanted were the advantages he lacked growing up—money, home, direction, respect—the four items missing in his father's makeup, disallowed by alcohol and Vietnam. To attain those things, Bragg had to become good at fabricating a self whose purpose is to achieve. Ironically, the more he achieved the more his persona grew. The more the culture validated his deeds, the more he grew into a self-making commodity—prizes for himself, inspiration for others.

A grown persona soon becomes mythic, the halo of male-pattern autobiography.

Wurtzel, by contrast, has no such course to follow. *Prozac Nation* is a book about careening through things psychically intangible, somewhere between honesty and pharmaceuticals. Is there any goal she has earned or persona she has become by the end? It's doubtful. All we know is that she is either less burdened or ready to start over. If anything, Wurtzel wants to rid herself of the young woman she is ashamed of, to *un*make herself and no longer be a selfish monster.

I like Bragg's many well-crafted scenes, his doing right by editor and mother. And I like much (though not all) of Wurtzel. But if our stories contain a moral code, I trust Wurtzel in a way that I don't trust Bragg. Indeed, about the only thing Wurtzel attains is an emotional trust in me, the reader. I trust her because she renders her story so fiercely, so flippantly, so like life. She mixes the past mess into the present mess, deceiving herself one day, unmasking her deception the next. Wurtzel unfurls the predicament: how can a young woman who is so emotionally transgressive also be so trustworthy? She resolves the predicament by balancing transgression and trust. Writers who work problems of trust into their memoirs are those for whom I and most of us have an affinity. It may sound crazy, but I tend to trust memoirists who embody the difficulty I and others have had in trusting them. It's in the troublesomeness of Wurtzel's trying to authenticate herself as someone I should trust that I feel closest to her.

13

The Trouble with Narrative

A Story's Tyranny

Since memoir is typically written as though it were a cousin to the novel, narrative is the form's chief stylistic device. We think that by making our stories narratively dramatic, we create emotional heat—the vaunted showing over the discouraged telling—that will catalyze the attention of readers. The nature of narrative is to set up expectations, then break or fulfill them. Writers accomplish this by using time-bending techniques of reduction, compaction, elision, foreshadowing, faster and slower pacing, rising and falling curves. The language of narration Erich Auerbach has defined as "an externalization of phenomena in terms perceptible to the senses" (6). The Homeric style, or realism, Auerbach says, began with the Greeks, whose "delight in physical existence [was] everything" (13). All authors know the importance of creating sensate characters whose external action, with life-and-death stakes, unfolds in detailed scenes. But no amount of realistic, dramatic narration will make a story personally revealing. In fact, the action-centered approach to memoir may be a crutch for memoirists, who (after reading Frank McCourt or Jeannette Walls) often believe that the drama memory tells about the past should, above all, infuse their writing.

In an earlier chapter, I talked of how memoirists alter factual and shape emotional truth—change names and locations; speed, slow, and summarize time; conjure via cloudy memory a snowstorm where one may not have been; and, once in a blue moon, completely change reality, as James Frey did in *A Million Little Pieces,* making a three-hour stint in jail into eighty-seven days (Frey should be given a Darwin award—*You:* Out of the gene pool!—for an easily traceable lie about his arrest record).[1] In 2003, according to *Salon,* Vivian Gornick told a group of students that she had "composed" conversations, invented scenes, and created composite characters in her memoir writing and (a few times) in her journalism (Sterling). In 2000, Gornick had written in *The Situation and the Story* that "in nonfiction the reader must believe that the narrator is speaking the truth. Of nonfiction it is invariably asked, 'Is this narrator trustworthy?'" (14). In response to the *Salon* story, Gornick denied "fabricating" anything. "I had made a composite out of the elements of two or more incidents . . . for the purpose of moving the narrative forward" (Gornick, "A Memoirist Defends Her Words"). Despite her defense, the cat was out of the bag.

Whether we dispute the meaning of "composed" versus "invented" versus "fabricated," the point is clear: moving the narrative forward is primary. Of course, the measure of a good story is whether we are "getting somewhere," as John Gardner wrote. But that doesn't mean there's only one method to get us there. Are the stylistic traits of fiction and epic and myth to be the stylistic traits of memoir? In my experience, nine out of ten memoirists will confess that they embellish their stories for dramatic effect. Nine out of ten will also admit that their memories of events have made their stories more dramatic than the original events themselves. Reading memoir, chunk by chunk in a group or finished in a book, I often feel writers adapting their material to the customs of narrative. Story transforms deed into lesson; story gets how to why in the least amount of time; story complicates and resolves. A good storyteller is always invited to the next party. A cynic might say that memoir must be story because it's the only avenue to a publisher's or a reader's approval. But the idea of casting your memoir into the narrative mold—in homage to other memoirists or in lieu of your own "form"—should be carefully considered. Emphasizing story won't activate the disclosure of self. Emphasizing story, in fact, may subordinate the disclosure of self to the tale. And while the fiction reader is supposed to trust the tale more than the teller, that adage doesn't fit memoir. To intermingle teller and tale, often in shifting times and shifting voices, is the goal. Which may mean that the writer gets in the way of the story. And for good reason.

Saying that memoir must be action-centered is like saying that poems must rhyme or symphonies must have contrasting movements. Whence came this idea? Publishers flock to narrative potboilers (fiction and nonfiction alike) because (we are told) audiences demand them: we want to know what it was like to be bedded by Michael Jackson and, just as critical, we want it told to us as story, not analysis. More troublesome is the fact that many memoirists, having internalized these conventions, write toward a form that they believe the literary culture has already anointed. The worst part of the Frey scandal is that the reading public may link narrative fabrication to all life-writing—biography, autobiography, and memoir. Readers think that parts of everyone's story *must* be made up. In order to be true, the unbelievable must co-star. This is the upshot of social control in a corporate society, which, massed at an electronic campfire, will believe almost anything it's told.

Not two decades into its emergence and diffusion at media warp speed, memoir may be irrevocably stamped as a fabricator's trade, undifferentiated from the novelist's. And yet this is not so. The form has no genre-like typology. Yet. (By writing this book I hope to clarify what memoir is as an antidote to its alleged fictional bias.) As I've said throughout, memoir in our time feels literarily unfixed. It has a grander, at times messianic, sense of itself and its possibilities by virtue not of what the publishers or the afternoon talk shows want but what the writers create.

Joseph Lelyveld: Breaking Free

In what case do we display such nondramatic, nontelegenic works as Mark Doty's memoir-cum-meditative-essay about seeing and painting, *Still Life with Oysters and Lemon* (2001), or Annie Dillard's utterly original *For the Time Being* (1999), a radical departure from her autobiography, *An American Childhood?* Dillard's book is a braided narrative that alternates ten disparate subjects (on Teilhard de Chardin, Israel, numbers, clouds, Chinese philosophy, and more) while keeping personal narrative to a minimum. And yet in these two books, things still feel memoiristic: Doty and Dillard begin in the neighborhood of self, family, and home but then wander off into subjects larger than what they know experientially—interests they expand with exposition and intensify with counterpointed themes. The memoiristic trusts the ungrounded. "This is a nonfiction first-person narrative," Dillard writes, "but it is not intimate, and its narratives keep breaking. Its form is unusual, its scenes are remote, its focus wide, and its tone austere. Its pleasures are almost purely mental" (ix). Texts like Dillard's stimulate readers to get somewhere via their associative abilities. Some assembly required; it's unlikely Oprah will call.

Consider Joseph Lelyveld's *Omaha Blues: A Memory Loop* (2005), a marvelous interrogation of memory written by a retired executive editor of the *New York Times*. With a reporter's zeal, Lelyveld pieces together the lives of his parents and a mentor when Lelyveld was young. As he tracks down who these three were—beyond his memory of them—the book brims with insights and reflects his maturity as person and journalist. Lelyveld is bedeviled by these elders: his rabbi father, a leader in Reform Judaism and the Zionist movement, who is a cold fish to his son; his mother, a beautiful woman with mental problems that stem, in part, from her disgust with marriage and motherhood; and Ben Goldstein, a rabbi, a member of the Communist Party, and a man, ten years older than the author, who takes Lelyveld to Yankees games and guides his development. Lelyveld still feels affection toward Ben, far more than he felt toward his uninvolved father. Distant parents, charismatic mentor. Of course, Lelyveld knew only bits and pieces of their actual lives while he knew them: he was too busy with his childhood and later his career, during which he was "shedding memories . . . as so much extra baggage" (3).

But as Lelyveld nears sixty, the past comes roaring back. The lives of his elders and his real and romantic feelings for them resemble a cold case, waiting in his memory and in archival vaults. (Lelyveld is lucky that his father's and Ben's lives were, in part, publicly recorded; investigating his mother's detachment is more difficult.) The truth Lelyveld is after is not something he's ashamed of or others have hidden in shame, though he does find the FBI's targeting of Ben, the radical rabbi, entirely unreasonable. Instead, the truth is assembled, ameliorated by the reporter's skill at writing the story "episodically." Thus, time and perception and place shift as he consults government files, news stories, and family letters as well as interviews friends. His hope, it seems, is to see how past events were linked in their time and how they compare with his memory and assessment now. Where such links are projected from now become alleyways Lelyveld haunts, running on hunches, tracking down leads. First he has to establish a framework for the past. Then his feelings about what he thought he felt and what he feels as he establishes that past can become the story.

Like a psychotherapist, Lelyveld gives credence to the process. The stability he seeks today will arrive, paradoxically, only by his staying on the merry-go-round of memory: "This is a memory loop, rather than a memoir; a particular circuit of memories that I feel driven to retrace and connect, where possible, to something like an objective record or the memories of someone else, in hopes of glimpsing what was once real." These loops, he says, "unravel" in his mind capriciously—that's how he thinks (18).

We might call Lelyveld's book a detective memoir. The object is not to solve a crime but, in combining personal and public memory, to solve past mysteries. Why did his mother hate marriage? Was Ben really a national security threat? Lelyveld spends hours unspooling microfilm to trigger recall of images and feelings that set him off on new excavations. For example, he's surprised to find that his youth wasn't as tumultuous as he had thought. Wasn't he miserable on the farm where his parents "exiled" him as a boy? He'd always figured he was sent away. But no. Once he retraces the event, by visiting the place and reading letters from the time, he finds he wasn't. He had imagined his abandonment; the scar he believed he had carried was a phantom. If one of his most coveted childhood memories mutated in the sunshine of archival exposure, what else had he misremembered? And why? "My surest, clearest memories," he writes, "had long since been heavily edited and now had to be revised" (21). Fact and feeling are revisable. This *aha* comes early: its efficacy shapes what follows. Along his "serpentine course" (14), there's a good deal of narrative history: era, context, the public record illuminating the private. Lelyveld, however, never lets go of his primal emotion—when fact and feeling collide, only honesty can sort out the wreckage.

Of memory's putative accuracy: "Yes, I was finding, it was possible to do a reporting job on your childhood, not to the point of total recall of course, but at least to a point where you could begin to see the cunning and willfulness of the selections on your own personal memory console" (23). Of his parents' marriage and divorce: "Any truism we utter about the impossibility of knowing what has gone on in a marriage must apply exponentially to the marriages of which we are the issues" (152). Of the selfishness of his search (anti-instinctual to a newspaperman): "None of what I'm discovering matters now to anyone in the world except me and Jo Rogers, Ben's daughter down in Knoxville, plus a couple of Goldstein nieces in California. But I sense I'm getting as close as I'll ever get to the core of a mystery that has fascinated me for more than half a century, the question of what drove Ben down his winding path to the point where I finally met him" (112–13).

Another crack in memory's crystal: Lelyveld had always felt pushed to follow his father to Mississippi in 1964 after his dad had been hurt as a civil rights activist during Freedom Summer. His memory of his father's character doesn't feel literarily full. "If this were a novel trying to get inside its characters, I'd feel compelled to supply my dad and myself with clear motives. But these often turn out to be untraceable in our lives as we happened to live them" (187). He comes upon a photograph of his father, who during a march was beaten severely by the police. The photo ran on the front pages of many American newspapers, a fact the author believes must have galvanized him into action: Wasn't he so moved by the sight that he set out at once to visit the hallowed ground of his father's wound? But the research he marshals says no. He didn't rush to Mississippi that year: an editor sent him to do a story. Again, so much of the past is serendipity, "bereft" of a "deeper motive." He writes, "I'd reinvent [a motive] if I weren't seeking to avoid reinvention here. As matters stand,

I'm left with the simple fact that I never set out to follow my dad" (189–90).

What is the emotional consequence of Lelyveld's looping? Should he hold himself accountable for deceiving himself about the importance of his father in his life? Should he be content with knowing now that his life has meaning only as "a tissue of happenstance" (189)? Lelyveld doesn't beat himself up over what he didn't realize may have been true. Nor does he apologize to a judge on the podium. Rather, he inhabits the edges of what he's culled. At times, his unraveling of the past is enough, self-evident in its finish. Other times, the edges do him in. At his father's funeral, Lelyveld hears his child's self calling, "'Daddy, Daddy, Daddy . . .' I've no idea whether there was a trace of memory in that scene imagined by the fifty-nine-year-old executive I'd somehow become. But I knew at once, as the service ran on and the little boy kept calling, that it was a feeling I'd suppressed practically all my life" (212).

Russell Baker writes in his review of *Omaha Blues* that "What we have here is a memoirist who distrusts memory, especially his own." Moreover, Lelyveld "deliberately shuns" what Baker calls the "fictional nature of the [memoir] form" (16). By researching his past and interrogating what he has found, Lelyveld has brewed more confusion than trauma, more intelligent doubt than narrative certainty. (By contrast, all of Frank McCourt feels traumatic and certain.) Confusion and doubt are rendered, in Lelyveld's example, without set dramatic scenes; rather, confusion and doubt are rendered with rumination and analysis—less taut but no less tangled. Lelyveld doesn't need to enlist memory's drama—he merely presents what he's remembered *and* reconstructed. Resisting its scenic engagement, he prizes the past for its evolving incompleteness. To emphasize that the past didn't happen as he thought it did is also to be honest with himself that he cannot refashion the past *as it was*. Lelyveld's contribution to the memoir form is existential and postmodern: there is no *as it was;* there is only our perspective now, interlocking with the past.

This may be the best question to ask ourselves as memoirists: What does my distrust of my memory and me—the narrator of memory—say about how I am choosing to represent myself and my story? I'm certain we all distrust our memories to some extent. But we compensate for the degree of distrust differently. A writer's compensation is that writer's memoir.

Further Liberation

I want to be clear: Lelyveld's work is not antinarrative, nor does he eschew narrative. Because he questions memory's and memoir's ability to tell the truth doesn't mean the resulting work is flat, or lacks profluence. Rather, he deemphasizes scenic narration and replaces it with nonfiction: fact, history, reportage, analysis, essay, reflection, assessment. Lelyveld insists that the memoir, like a circus train, carry all these. His does and he keeps stoking the fire, mostly by sheer will and by his desire to know (which is to write) the truth. In Lelyveld's hands, the memoir is pliant—telling and assessing story, trusting and distrusting memory. Such possibility liberates Lelyveld, as it does the majority of contemporary memoirists. They, we, are captivated by the content and the nature of recollecting. We're willing to subvert the reader's expectation of the well-crafted story, especially when the writing brings us to the individual character of our memories.

As memoir develops, we're seeing more writers questioning the preponderance of narrative. Their underlying query is, How much should my life's exploits be dramatized? How do I choose and pace the amount of reflection or narrative that's appropriate to my story? What can I learn from other writers? McCarthy and Fraser, Doty and Eggers, Karr and O'Faolain, Wurtzel and Lelyveld each activate new ways of voicing and structuring their stories.

They write reflective self-analysis that also transports a reader emotionally. They combine and recombine techniques of narrative and exposition endlessly. They pit remembering and remembered selves against each other. Through trial and error, they get somewhere, often somewhere new.

The question of narrative degree is also a question of genre and memoir. Genre suggests a literary categorization based on traits. For instance, in the postmodern fiction of Thomas Pynchon or David Foster Wallace we note the self-conscious parodic voice, the fragmented narrative, the hyperenergetic sprawl. In contemporary memoir, we see books labeled by subject (which is to say, labeled by publisher): childhood, coming-of-age, love-life, sex life, family, travel, life phase, and so on. It should be obvious that we're not close to labeling memoir by style, such as narrative, sudden, detective, assembled, or reflective, forms I've been naming and discussing.

Still, some writers seek the safety of categories, of models, of how-to. Here's a scenario. A student is working on a memoir about depression. He asks, Should I follow one of the two most recognized and sober books on the disease, Kay Redfield Jamison's *An Unquiet Mind: A Memoir of Moods and Madness* (1995) or William Styron's *Darkness Visible: A Memoir of Madness* (1990)? Sure, I say, read them; models can help orient you. But note how dissimilarly each author shapes the hyperbolic thing we call "madness": Jamison's book is relational and dynamic, pinnacled on her manic highs and depressive lows, in episodes with lovers and with her work as a medical student and psychiatrist; Styron's is wall-to-wall analysis with an unfeeling, diagnostic, pallid tone. These tales are right by their authors. Form follows function; memoir follows personality; the unique life is the unique memoir.

There's another element to which memoirists are reacting. From Virginia Woolf to Joan Didion, the memoirist has learned that the narrating self must be portrayed differently than a narrating character in fiction. This is no scholarly claim: the novelist/memoirist, who's written in both realms, attests to the behavioral gap between I as character and I as author. Among the best double threats in prose, along with Geoffrey Wolff, Kathryn Harrison, Frank Conroy, Mary Gordon, and John Edgar Wideman, is Alice Sebold. Her memoir, *Lucky* (1999), the story of her rape at nineteen, was published before her novel, *The Lovely Bones* (2002), the story of the rape and murder of a fourteen-year-old girl who is not Sebold. She began writing the rape-and-murder tale first but then stopped. Here's her explanation, from an interview: "I think that after writing the first chapter of *Lovely Bones,* in which Susie is raped and killed, there was some urging on Susie's part that I get my own business out of the way before writing further into her story. When I say 'on Susie's part' I mean: the demands of her wanting to tell her story and using me to do so meant that I had to unload *my story* someplace else. It wasn't going to fit into the book I wanted to write for her."

Though the phrase "unload my story" suggests it was secondary or in the way, Sebold's act was hardly opportunistic. Both books are scenic narrative; however, she was able to resist writing a fictionalized autobiography of rape because the memoir form (again I stress its usefulness) was available as a kind of active literary resistance. Sebold—with Susie's insistence—distrusted her memoir and fiction writing selves equally. Those selves also seemed to distrust each other. To her credit, Sebold listened. Further in the interview Sebold remarks that friends in California "pressed me to write my story, I think because they realized that if I did that my fiction would be cleaner and better on the other side." She says, too, that were she to have fictionalized her rape it would have been a "veiled experience." "I went straight to memoir," she says, and memoir removed the veil.

Though author and theme are the same, the two rapes are uniquely described and felt by their narrators. This is Sebold's triumph. Fiction and memoir become synergistic—not in a single book but as complements. When memory insists that *this must be remembered,* it is also saying that *this must be memoir.* With memoir an option, writers can reinscribe something *other* about the self in fiction. The standard adage about writing what you know in a novel no longer applies. The writer today is treatment-minded: she can assess how she wants to write the truth—imaginatively in fiction, personally in memoir. In fact, because of memoir's emergence, any writer can now separate the masks and the selves of authorship. Memoir has freed the author from having to choose between how much the self should or shouldn't be fictionalized.

The idea is to get away from fiction's narrative presentation of character and get closer to memoir's reflective presentation of self. I think memoir is differentiating itself from fiction because it has to evolve as its own literary form. Autobiography first, the memoir now, have grown out of and away from the storytelling traditions of myth, epic, and fiction. Memoir is individualizing, self-actualizing, if you like, finding its personality while still sharing some of the style and rhetoric of fiction. Moreover, the memoirist seeks to know himself by individualizing that self—but not for ego alone. There is social purpose to adult development. Anthony Stevens, in a splendid biography, *On Jung,* quotes the psychologist's assertion that "'a human being would certainly not grow to be seventy or eighty years old if this longevity had no meaning for the species.'" Stevens writes that Jung—who was himself an essayistic memoirist in *Memories, Dreams, Reflections* (1963)—believed "the function of people in the second half of life is to sustain the culture that supported their youth." And, Stevens continues, "By following the archetypal imperative to individuate, we become as complete human beings as we can *within the context of our culture* and, in so doing, perform our highest spiritual function for the well-being of society as well as for the personal fulfilment of our lives" (185; emphasis in original).

Some argue that to write memoir or to seek individuation (à la Jung's practice) is a purely selfish enterprise. Hardly. Personal fulfillment and the longevity of life are evolutionary imperatives. If you look at any index of human development (such "quality of life" measures, like the one used by the United Nations, must balance tangible and intangible criteria)—child welfare, health care, democratic institutions, political freedom, human rights, psychological wellness, environmental well-being, life expectancy, meaningful work, the arts—you find that social and personal betterment are mutually dependent. It may be that the desire for individual fulfillment is what predominantly drives a society to evolve.

14

The World the Self Inherits

James McBride: Mother, Race, Memoir

Memoir tells of how we relate to a past and how a past relates to us during the time—the ever-nagging present—in which we write our stories. Along the way, authentic and inauthentic selves interact: a writer tries to find who is the private me that the public me has covered over. Another kind of relationship that compels the memoir writer is between an author and that which is largely outside him. Call this outsider an *other* and place the other in a realm of its own. How often it is that this other arrives in our lives as a *memoir-making* force. Mary Karr's mother's depression. The deaths of Dave Eggers's parents. My father's contradictory authority. Things that burden us, which haunt or oppose us in ways we cannot defend against, let alone avoid. Some of the best tales about ourselves we find have come *for* us, washed ashore in the wreckage of others' lives and others' traditions. What is beached—a set of biracial parents, a culture's disapproval of homosexuality—one day insists that we start picking through it.

Many write memoir because they are transformed by a power or a person greater than the self. This power is seldom supernatural, and yet it is not easily explained. We are not exactly passive in the relationship. But there is a sense that when the memoir-making force chooses us, we must organize. We must separate what we've felt from what we've observed others have felt, and see our lives in context. For instance, my father's unevenly applied authority toward me and my brothers during childhood. His authority is largely outside me: I see him order my brothers around with less severity than he orders me, and, growing up, I don't understand why. I feel different than how I witness my brothers feel. His favoritism haunts me. Push this into the world. Because of his example at home, I experience school, neighborhood, adults—and their uneven authority—differently than my brothers do. They, too, internalize their treatment as special and inconsistent but also unfair. My life feeds into theirs. I try to find a balance: I am a self and a son and a brother; I interact with my father's commands in ways my brothers don't; I grapple with the unequal codes of discipline from school, neighborhood, era. Thus, in the writing I attempt, how my father shapes me is different from how my father shapes my brothers, which, in turn, is different from how my school and community shape me and them.

All these things jostle for position until one day I discover that writing about my father is not only *my* struggle with his authority, it is also, perhaps more, the ways in which the advantaged and disadvantaged experiences of those close to me have shaped my struggle with the culture of authoritarianism. I have to see my years under the paternal and community thumb as mine, and my brothers' as theirs; and I have to see that there was much in my father and in the culture of the 1950s that created me and the way

I relate to authority. Why does all this *otherness* matter? Because the maturity of authorship has shown me that it's not all about me—even in the memoir.

THIS SORTING OF SELF and other lies at the core of James McBride's *The Color of Water: A Black Man's Tribute to His White Mother* (1996). McBride's purpose is apparent in the subtitle: what she endured has to be told so that what he endured can be comparatively appreciated. McBride alternates chapters: she tells her story and he tells his. (Her story is the result of his transcribing and organizing her reminiscences.) Ruth's tale focuses on her parents' lives, her Jewish upbringing, her father's sexual and emotional abuse, her escape to Harlem, her marriage to McBride's father, and her raising twelve children. At one point, she says (her words are in italics), "*I stayed on the black side because that was the only place I* could *stay. The few problems I had with black folks were nothing compared to the grief white folks dished out*" (232). McBride's story reacts to his mother's: he tells of his bewilderment with this woman who, unlike all other whites he observes, chooses to live in the black community. And he goes further. Unlike her, he wants to understand the connection between their different colors. After all, what he knows about her is mostly wrong or uninformed. Ashamed of her past, overwhelmed by a dozen kids, she's never told him the truth of her past during his youth. To get it down, McBride cajoles her. But it takes years to force this black-community, biracial, Christian-Jewish, personal story out. Or it may the opposite. The black community, his biracial identity, the Christian church, the Jewish synagogue, and his mother cajole him to write *his* story, which is *their* story. The memoir-making force chooses him. I am my community. My community is me. And yet, despite the magnanimity he showers on his mother, it takes a self-revealing author, and a persevering one at that, to get it down right.

Given these generational, racial, and religious elements, it's no wonder that the self McBride discloses in the book is a self he doesn't know himself to be until the memoir spells it out for him. Here's how he voices himself in four separate self-disclosures, moments of insight into his personal identity:

> Yet I myself had no idea who I was. I loved my mother yet looked nothing like her. Neither did I look like the role models in my life—my stepfather, my godparents, other relatives—all of whom were black." (91)

> I *had* to find out more about who I was, and in order to find out who I was, I had to find out who my mother was." (266)

> It was a devastating realization, coming to grips with the fact that all your life you had never really known the person you loved the most." (266)

> It was a fascinating lesson in life history—a truth-is-stranger-than-fiction marvel, to say the least. I felt like a Tinkertoy kid building my own self out of one of those toy building sets; for as she laid her life before me, I reassembled the tableau of her words like a picture puzzle, and as I did, so my own life was rebuilt." (269–70)

You can hear the urban renewal motifs of tearing down and building up. He realizes that what was unknown and false was favored. He lingers on the falsity of this favoring to destroy it. He reassembles new selves: one for his mother, in her own words, which—surprise!—reassembles *him*. All this is accomplished because McBride listened to Ruth, the woman she was, in part, before she became his mother. Having heard, he lets *her*—mother and woman—in on *his* memoir. (Many who read this book are struck that Ruth's life is more vital than her son's. One reason is that he is slow to catch on to the beastly racial prejudices that she endured and he can only imagine.)

McBride highlights one of his mother's stories, how she would place crumbs on the ledge of her window, where birds would gather and she would sing to them. Later, she would shoo them away with the Yiddish song "Birdie, Birdie, Fly Away" (218). This is Ruth's theme—caring for someone in such a way that the person is encouraged one day to leave. The fly-away theme is dramatized twice: first, when McBride is being bused to camp, and his mother is there, outside the bus's window, standing next to a Black Panther, whom McBride fears because they hate white people and his mother is white; and second, when McBride leaves on a bus for college and his mother sees him off: "As I sat down on the bus and looked for her through the window, it occurred to me that since I was a little boy, she had always wanted me to go" (189). Going is what Ruth had to do in childhood—to escape her sexually abusive, guilt-inducing, racist father. She passes on the value of emptying the nest, whether it's by a gentle or a hurtful nudge.

It's clear that McBride has tried to fit himself into his mother's heritage. He reports this as his purpose early on: "As a boy, I never knew where my mother was from—where she was born, who her parents were. When I asked she'd say, 'God made me.' When I asked if she was white, she'd say, 'I'm light-skinned,' and change the subject. . . . It took me fourteen years to unearth her remarkable story . . . and she revealed it more as a favor to me than out of any desire to revisit the past" (xvii). Fourteen years is some dedication. Many readers wonder whether in placing Ruth and the black-white issue center stage destines the book to be a racial biography more than an individual memoir. (Some have called this form a family memoir.) Are McBride's relationships—he and his culture, he and his mother, he and his racial identity—too many? Has he resolved them? Does he still possess a *self* by the book's end? Having left home, he, too, could have stayed away; he didn't need to investigate. But it is McBride's genius (he is part memoirist, part journalist, like Joseph Lelyveld) that insists he disclose himself through the other, that is, his mother's tale. The self he has become by writing the book is one who is not enslaved or hoodwinked by his tradition of family folklore. It speaks of the hunt, of dogged determination. The act of getting his mother's story on paper, at times against her better judgment, is tantamount to family liberation.

Some of the best writing occurs when McBride, in his late twenties, finds and interviews people who knew Ruth when she was a girl, pre-Harlem. Told of their remembrances, Ruth fills out the details and more willingly participates in her son's project. In those passages we are touched by the author's pleasure in overturning the legacy of family silence. It's a family memoir about a very tight-lipped family. McBride wants to change the pattern and end the not-knowing, the unawareness, the ignorance, the dried-up myths that most families are inured to. Placing her words next to his—he needs her voice as much as she needs his—gives the book its munificence. It's a duet for mother and son, his and her solos, a two-part invention.

Delusions Disclosed

In "Never Trust a Memoirist," Stacy Schiff writes about Benjamin Franklin and his sojourn to France late in life. She says that contemporary memoir "bursts" with "qualities" that would have never feathered Franklin's quill. Today, these qualities—"self-aggrandizement, self-pity, self-justification, self-consciousness, self-reflection, self-delusion"—"seem to impel a person to compose [memoir] in the first place" (66). Of this hyperbolic self, Schiff sounds dismissive. But, despite her grievance, she's tapped a vein. To present the self as a consequence of one's deeds is the work of autobiography, certainly of Franklin's. To present the self as a person disclosing the mutability of the self is the work of memoir, certainly in recent literary history. Let's say a writer hopes to tell of how he once, in a particular phase of his life, deluded himself. He is the "I" who can tell the story of self-delusion. The author must show us who he was. But to disclose who he was, he must no longer be delusional. Sounds easy. It's not. To disclose old and new selves—the formerly deluded person who is now undeluded—requires a purgative agent, a *contending* other.

Memoirists have their special interests—to be self-aggrandizers, to be self-deluders, to be self-celebrants. But we all must self-disclose, that is, reveal the person memoir-writing has made us. Some authors believe that the person we reveal is an enlarged being, far more aware of self and world, self and other, than when we began. What could be bigger as a memoirist than the force of my family coursing through me, particularly once I set sail on the sea of my emotion, my memory, my fact? What else is James McBride's bigness but that which his family, his race, his community have worked out through him *as* him, an aggregate self. McBride's self-disclosure is that he's a collective discloser, and this course marks a significant new direction that the memoir form is taking. Meanwhile, there are memoirists who are doing what Schiff abhors— writing candid books that are narcissistic, incorrigible, opaque. In fact, some writers think that readers want to hear only what's unusual about them, to hear the outrageous, because we've not lived it, along with the absurd, the obscene, the exaggerated: here we are now, entertain us; through you, let us dare.

How easy it is to confuse candor with self-disclosure. The result—if no *other* is present—is masturbation. Literally, in one case. An obsessional love of anal sex characterizes Toni Bentley's *The Surrender: An Erotic Memoir* (2004). What impels the book is her desire to show us that she has achieved "emancipation through the back door" (7). True, there's as much salaciousness in her sodomy as there is in our reading about it. But the book lacks that contentious other—either a reflective voice that contrasts with her gritty sex talk or an actual concern for another person (her partners exist only below the waist, decapitated as it were). In short, without an other, the thrill becomes a bore. Grandstanding sexual addiction (almost all of it takes place in her bedroom), the memoir moves with tedious, repetitious, cutesy detail. Anal sex is not oppositional in the way Bentley thinks it is, the "back side" of some personal vaginal hangup, which, she says, all women have. Her prior other—her non-anal-sex self, before the coming of "A-Man," her savior, who "frees" her—is a "bad marriage" to the "great love of my life," followed by "poor choices" in "Paul Newman–like" "boyfriends" (41). Nor is there a self within that takes shape as a result of her new sex life. Who cares that she finds paradise in her sphincter? Who cares that she numbers the encounters with A-Man all the way to 298? If she doesn't care about anything more than her bum, why should we? Without a foil for her gushing about the physical and aesthetic beauty of sodomy, hallowing it works only to enslave, not to liberate, her. No context exists— love, regret, loss, a literature of the anal-erotic, non-anal intimacy with others—that would bring any meaning beyond an addictive pleasure. A passion spent on itself is one quickly spent.[1]

A delusional self-obsession is, for the memoirist, the hardest other to capture—in part because a self-obsession is beyond one's control. To disclose the delusion the self has lived under takes real skill. Consider Lauren Slater's *Lying: A Metaphorical Memoir* (2000). Slater's other is genetically set: she has epilepsy and seizures and (perhaps) Munchausen's syndrome; she also has depression, a plight she detailed in *Prozac Diary*. Prozac helped her become a psychologist and a renowned writer. But her childhood and adolescence were imperiled by epileptic disorders: "Epilepsy is a fascinating disease," Slater writes, in command of her delusion, "because some epileptics are liars, exaggerators, makers of myths and high-flying stories" (6). Some like her.

Enter the trapeze artist and three instances of deft lying. First, as a victim of seizures, Slater discovers that she can use them to confound and betray others, usually her mother: one day in a supermarket, her mother tries to stop Lauren physically from having a seizure, but witnesses call the police and Lauren is taken away, a victim of "abuse," and her mother is detained. Second, at seventeen, Slater lies her way into being accepted at the Bread Loaf Writers' Conference and there is bedded by a literary star, who is not named: the lengthy scene pulses with a tit-for-tat romance seducer and seduced adjoin. And third, seeking a social cure, Slater joins Alcoholics Anonymous on the pretense that she's a drinker. She's not. Whenever she fesses up to her dissembling and tells them that she's not an alcoholic, they respond with applause and tears: Oh, yes, that's so true, that's what we all say, that's why we're here, to stop the denial.

Throughout are Slater's peppered-in asides, suggesting that she may be lying or misremembering: "This I think I recall" (24); "I admit I sometimes faked my epilepsy, but I also really had it" (91); "Sometimes, I don't even know why the facts should matter. I often disregard them, and even when I mean to get them right, I don't" (145); and this note from her memo to Random House, her publisher, on how to market *Lying:* "The neural mechanism that undergirds the lie is the same neural mechanism that helps us make narrative. Thus, all stories, even those journalists swear up and down are 'true,' are at least physiologically linked to deception" (164). Slater's a fledgling discloser, learning what to confess and what to leave alone. To alleviate her shame, whose hold on her is really the theme of the book, she meets with her surgeon, Dr. Neu. Several years earlier, Neu had completed five operations in her brain that partially severed right and left hemispheres and helped end most of Slater's auras and seizures. His response to her is, "Okay . . . you lied. But really, Lauren, I don't want you to feel guilty. In one sense you lied, but in another sense you didn't, because trickery is so hinged to your personality style, and, therefore, you were only being true to yourself" (202).

There's overindulgence here in dramatizing exaggeration and then rationalizing it by writing, Yes, it's true that epileptics exaggerate and rationalize. In addition, Slater's narrator sounds unreliable, a voice whose authenticity I wonder about. Is it possible to be an unreliable narrator of memoir? On one hand, no. If she's undeluding herself, she must be reliable. On the other hand, as Dr. Neu maintains, lying is the donnée. Like Elizabeth Wurtzel, Slater is diseased with inauthenticity. But she's also writing memoir as a means of recovery. The honest-duplicitous world must be processed, especially as it acts through Slater's epilepsy. Not only does she respond in kind, but she also admits regularly to honesty *and* duplicity, to her chameleonic part in it all. "This is my tale and I have written it over and over again, and, depending on my mood and my auras, the story always seems to change, and yet it always seems true" (158). Slater emphasizes her relationships with others to disclose this dual manipulation. Lying takes two. And for the liar, whether it's genetically set or not, the guilt can be as heavy as the redemption.

This is what's so hard about memoir: you may disclose the self who's figured it out, who's aware of having changed or been changed, who has survived. But that self may still not be aware of its ability to dissemble. Self-disclosure means disclosing the truth to yourself at the same time that you disclose it to your readers. To trust an author fully is to feel the authenticity of this truth in the author, who is disclosing it to herself at the same time she is waking up to it.

Boy of Steel: *Coming Out and Coming In*

A few years ago, Steve entered my memoir-writing class, wanting, as he says, "to figure out how the form worked because I knew at some point I would write the story of my life." That story entails his growing up gay in decidedly ungay Pocatello, Idaho, and revealing his sexual nature slowly and painfully to his friends, his parents, and himself. He began writing his story after his mother died. Though very close to her, he thought that her death would free him. It has and it hasn't. He still fears her judgment as much as he does reliving in writing the pain of her illness and death. And yet her death did free him to write, at least circumspectly, about how he was not allowed to reveal his core self to anyone. It was forbidden by a set of Cub Scout traditions, on which he was bred and to which he adapted. He played the role of the "straight boy" to parents and friends. To relive the faux straight-boy self, a sham of the gay person he knew he was, has been stressful. "I was scared about the idea of being true to my experience. I've struggled with that: what is being true to your experience and your memory? That scared me because I felt an obligation—in terms of telling the truth—that I felt I could not live up to. Either I would be unable to reveal certain 'secrets' or my memory would fail me."

He continues. "I had no idea that I would write about some of the things I've ended up writing about; I do think I went deeper and deeper because I trusted that this writing group was not going to be judgmental about or uncomfortable with what I was writing." The subject of gay sex, particularly the actual physical sex between boys, he says, is uncomfortable for everyone. He also wondered, "Am I publishing a gay memoir or am I publishing a memoir? I'm interested in appealing to a broader audience."

Amy is Steve's oldest, dearest friend, also a one-time girlfriend who had "to painfully find out that I was gay." She has asked Steve to write the scene where the two of them, as teenagers, tried to have sex. In a hotel room in Jackson Hole, Wyoming, he says, "I failed the test. I could not do it. I had already had many gay experiences but she didn't know that." At the time, it was his attempt "to get rid of this thing called 'being gay.' It's an important story in my life—I've tried but I can't quite write it. I don't want to hurt her; I want to tell the story truthfully, be generous in the way I tell it. And she keeps saying to me, 'You can't hurt me, no matter what. We're too close.'"

The story of Amy and him is emblematic of the legacy of Steve's hiddenness. For example, he knows he's writing about his childhood as a way *not* to write about his mother's death. "Could I write about her death? Yes. But could I write about it better after I've taken more time emotionally with it? Yes. It's much easier for me to write about people who are not in my life or who are not alive to judge what I've written."

Here is Steve's first lesson in what he's disclosed to himself so far. "Those around me who would judge me"—which includes his recently deceased mother—"make the writing harder." His work reflects his acceptance and avoidance of those subjects and relationships whose judgment he still feels—like Amy, like his mother, like admitting to sex with boys. And yet that judgment, in a sense, keeps him from disclosing the truth. It's a paradox. Were that judgment to evaporate, would he then be able to disclose more? Maybe, maybe not. What he knows now is that he can only tell so much. Put another way, self-disclosure can be full (and fully difficult) even in its tentative and managed stages. The disclosure of some authors may not be much in absolute terms, but personally it is enormous, perhaps costly. (This give-and-take has Steve organizing his book, *Boy of Steel,* as discrete stories. The idea comes from Bernard Cooper's *Maps to Anywhere* [1990]: to reveal things in serial or semiconnected units. The putative assurance of a thematic chronology won't do: he wants the reader to assemble his life as he himself has had to.)

An epigraph for his story is a line from the song "Deconstruction," by the Indigo Girls: "We're sculpted from youth / The chipping away makes me weary." "What I started as was an innocent human being. All along the way, people just kept chipping away at me. You can't do this, you can't say that, you can't dream this. I was worn down to the point of wanting to commit suicide when I was young. I stood in front of the mirror in my parents' bathroom with pills and wondered what I should do." That is, until a high school friend killed herself. "Her death helped me get beyond that thinking because I saw how selfish it was. Having got beyond that, being able to accept myself and express myself—that's the story for me."

One nagging element for him has been to understand the mask that a boy who knows he's gay must wear. "The way I understood the mask was simply that there were lots of secrets I needed to keep hidden. The more positive I was, the more pleasant I was, the more I excelled at things, the more those spotlights would take attention away from the possibility that other people would find what those secrets were. That's how I perceived it as a young man. Dorian Gray. There is this darker self that was not good; anybody who knew about it would think I was a horrible person."

Trying to please his father with the boy things—football, golf, fishing—caused problems because Steve didn't excel at them. "I gave up on him early on. It was really my mother. These were the things she wanted me to do. She wanted me to play saxophone, I played saxophone. She wanted me to be stellar in conversation in adult company, so I was. She needed me to tell her how much I loved her and give back the affection she showed me, honoring birthdays and holidays, so I did." His father didn't give his mother the kind of attention she wanted. So it devolved to Steve. To please her was double duty: to make up for his father and to hide himself even more.

In addition to his parents, how obvious was it to others that he was over-pleasing them? "I didn't care whether they thought I was being genuinely this or that—so long as they didn't know I was this other thing. To whatever degree they didn't believe my act, as long as they believed most of it, I was happy." One way of coping was theater. There, role-playing suited him. "The pleaser would get the accolades, and I pleased a lot of people. As long as I got that applause and attention back, that's what nurtured me. The lasting damage of that—what my therapist says—is that I'm always seeking attention outwardly. I never did develop self-acceptance or self-love. That was the part that was missing. I always hated myself inside and thought I was awful. Anything that people gave me in terms of attention and applause—I always knew was false. I always knew I didn't deserve it. Because I was acting."

Steve considered his acting to be, for a time, his authenticity. It let him pretend to be his "natural self"—to adopt roles in which he could express his romantic sensibility. But "it wasn't the whole story. If others knew the whole story," which his frightened self kept suppressed, "then the whole house of cards would come tumbling down. I really wasn't pleasing myself, I was pleasing others. To me the things I wanted to do to please myself were mostly dark secrets. Those were the things I'd really like to do. That boy over there: I had to pretend not to want him, but I really would have loved to be with him."

Steve intends to write about the moment he discovered that "what *my* natural impulses were, were not natural to others. I was sexually active about age nine with this boy next door. It was the greatest thing in the world. And then one day, when I wanted to do what we'd always done, which is fool around, he said, 'We can't do that anymore. We're going into junior high and we have to be going after girls.' Clearly he had changed. He was telling me that what I wanted was unnatural. It was a phase, and I needed to grow out of it. And that's when I found, 'Oh, really. I thought this would go on forever.' I had pictured this as my natural self."

Given competition between his internal and external selves, he ran the gauntlet between rejecting and holding onto them. He rejected the natural self as others around him did so he might survive socially. And yet he also held on to his natural self. That natural self is the boy who felt he'd go on forever *and* told himself to repress his homosexuality. He was always caught in this dilemma—repressing but only partially; revealing but only partially. That is, until his natural self won out (or walked away from the ruins) as a man and, later, as a memoir writer. That natural self has also been repressed and unburdened by gays and lesbians who were, in part, raised to be homophobic and had to seek clandestine ways to be themselves, and by a society that was protecting its gender authority at the same time it was unlearning its prejudices. Though ostracized as an individual and as gay, Steve still had to adapt to the straight world of Pocatello, Idaho. But unless that world begins listening and adapting to him, there can be no collective disclosure with which Steve and other homosexuals might engage.

"I want people to see my individual story," he says. "But I also want people to see us [gays and lesbians] as a group of people differently, understand us more, be able to see us more in their own lives. I like that. I have been politically active a lot. But I think you change people's minds when they understand it not at an activist level but at an emotional one."

As both *The Color of Water* and Steve's writing about his adolescence have revealed, we cannot undelude the world which has raised us. The best we can do is undelude ourselves.

15

A Memoir Culture

From Explosion to Backlash and Back

Working to undelude the self, or at least working to become less deluded, is memoir's payoff, a change that we feel in the teller because of the story's action. Readers root for some awareness that the journey has altered, perhaps liberated, the writer. When the payoff is revealed—felt in the writing and recognized by the author—we judge the work honest, emotionally worthy. But can the personal payoff extend itself in any way to the culture or the generation from which the writer has come? Can the memoirist show that his culture or society is malleable like him? Can a memoir, a personal document, stand for what groups of people endure? How is memoir's voice crucial to the time and place in which it is written? And is all of this relational linking between culture and self only the memoirist's responsibility? These are far-ranging questions for a new literary form.

On the publication of *My Life in the Middle Ages: A Survivor's Tale* (2005), biographer-turned-memoirist James Atlas wondered whether his book fit today's standard for the memoir. He said in an interview that the books "I've been following lately usually involve being beaten up by one's parents or other dysfunctional crises. I've had my problems but nothing dramatic enough for a memoir. I wanted to write about people in our generation and what I hoped was our common experience" (Mehegan). In Atlas's assessment, I find a trace of the backhanded compliment. Unless the story is imbued with dysfunction, an author should hoist a mea culpa: beware, readers, few indignities of my wretched self this way come. Atlas seems to suggest that for any new memoir, the curvature of its hell-and-back journey has been prescribed. To veer from that plot line requires explanation. Fearing we'll peg his memoir to the trauma index, he'd rather we judge it by a cultural criterion: does Atlas adequately, that is, dramatically, reveal the social and cultural values with which his generation produced him *in the absence of* a family crisis?

To find out, you'll have to read the book. But short of that, Atlas's query is valuable. To think that memoir must always involve family-based crises is, at best, uninformed. (An agent in the early 1990s told me that only if my memoir about my father featured harrowing physical abuse could the book be sold to an editor.) There are exceptional books by Christopher Hudson, Annie Dillard, Alec Wilkinson, and Craig Seligman that obviate family tragedy in favor of intellectual, reflective, even investigatory tacks. In some of these books, the emotional terror may be more imagined than lived. The fear-pride spectrum of the United States Marine recruit is the subject of Anthony Swofford's *Jarhead* (2003). Swofford is not induced to write by what he suffers in his family (which is minor) but by his own fantasies of death and self-worth as the Marines convert him into a sniper. His training taps his already puffed-up craving to kill—and to feel less than a man if he's not allowed to prove himself. Which is his fate, for he faces negligible combat during the Persian Gulf War.

Atlas is right to be wary of memoir-as-trauma. Lest we forget, alongside the "memoir explosion" of the last decade, we've also had the "memoir backlash." The explosion was borne along by the avidity of writers and readers and (some) publishers while the backlash emanated from querulous critics and overworked editors. Zoe Heller, who wrote widely about memoir in the late 1990s, thought the typical specimen was a "lyrical, ever-so-writerly account of a lousy childhood involving incest, physical abuse, alcoholism, poverty, anorexia, bulimia, drug addiction, [or] sexual perversity." Heller notes that by 1998 she was "memoired-out," tired of the "vertiginous standards of modern exhibitionism," tired of the "modish, scandalous confessions of recent years."

Many critics, including Atlas, figured authors who'd written of abominable lives had come out for therapy, for money, for conformance—but not for art and certainly not for honesty. Atlas was merely counterpunching against what he assumed most memoirists were up to. (I often wonder whether critics *read* memoir or merely parrot what reporters in *Publishers Weekly* write about the form.) So he summoned his historical orientation— write about his culture and his generation, much as Alfred Kazin had done in his three autobiographical volumes. Atlas has said something vital: we do indulge family and the squirming-free self as the centerpieces of our memoirs. The relationship between self and generation (or self and the natural world, self and the economy; the possibilities are endless) is every bit as valid as that between self and family. Such relatedness may be less fraught, but it's no less valid.

To get out of the cloister of their lives, Joseph Lelyveld emphasized the conflict between his apolitical reporting and his father's radicalism; so, too, did James McBride, who breached the levee between his blackness and his mother's whiteness. For James

Atlas, personal and cultural sensitivities unite in a targeted audience. Clearly, the generational card has seldom been played in memoir, perhaps for good reason. On the one hand, we think that any memoirist is a product of her era, and thus her book is inherently critical of that era. On the other hand, we think because the subject is the self, the era is or should be relegated to the backseat. But I would argue that this simple divide limits a memoir's potential. Culture and generation as much as individual experience instruct memory, no matter how much the writer may ignore or sublimate those larger contexts in the writing. The *New York Times*'s critic Margo Jefferson concurs: "The problem [with memoir] is figuring out how to examine and dramatize ourselves without forgetting to pay the same attention to the larger historical and spiritual forces that have made us." It's a question of balance: *the same attention.*

Moreover, this rapprochement between culture and self has been missing, in part because the memoir has ripened so quickly. Once memoir gains mainstream acceptance, like the novel or the film, its currency—each memoir speaks to the time of its writing—will be better integrated into each individual's tale. So far, memoirists have been predominantly past-centered. Ideas such as how the culture or a generation pushes a writer to remember the past remain untapped. One new land to explore is the meeting between self-consciousness and political or religious belief. I have no doubt that such undertakings will come. To date, though, there are too few under-forty authors who are using memoir to chastise and celebrate their generational selves. Such essayistic memoirists— Meghan Daum, Dave Eggers, Sarah Vowell, Sean Wilsey, to name four—write about nineties and two thousands angst in a voice whose arch and caustic humor readers love. Above all, it's this voice of a new class of writers that captivates us. Voicing how the self and the culture internalize each other is, I think, where the memoir is headed.

The Voice of a Generation

A new voice-dominated class of memoir writers—which I'll discuss momentarily—is possible only because the form has been born in a particular generation. Memoir's rise during the last twenty years mirrors the maturation of those Americans born between 1946 and 1964, the era of the Baby Boom. During memoir's rise, Elvis buffs and Cold War hipsters turned forty and fifty. Not only are boomers writers (classes I teach are packed with their stress-laden faces), but their numbers will grow as they retire. More will devote more time to the practice, authoring tales of personal fulfillment tempered by regret and spirituality. Much as James Atlas has.

The culture has bred into boomer sensibility the value of the author's growth, at any age. For the older group, this means adapting to aging as opposed to letting age overtake them. The idea that an adult develops psychically, just as a child develops physically, is traceable to Carl Jung. Jung believed that all people were capable of individualizing but, for a host of reasons, very few ever got there. They simply ran out of time. "Many—far too many—aspects of life," Jung writes, "which should also have been experienced lie in the lumber-room among dusty memories . . . glowing coals under grey ashes." One way we run out of time is by ignoring our core desires. We suppose our social adaptations to be "eternally valid" while we "make a virtue of unchangeably clinging to them" (72). Robert Bly, in *A Little Book on the Human Shadow*, is also critical of the Jekyll-and-Hyde split in the civilized human psyche: "How did the two persons get separated? Evidently we spend the first twenty or twenty-five years of life deciding what should be pushed down in the shadow self, and the next forty years trying to get in touch with that material again" (64). Our neuroses, which may intensify in later life, galvanize us to reexamine ourselves. With therapist in tow, we might reach Jung's individuation or Erik Erikson's final stage of growth, "ego integrity."

As economic monads, defined by our consumption, many of us fifty-and-over have entrenched ourselves in attitudes, positions, personae that ensure security and conformity. In the process, we have neglected the self's demands for creativity and adaptation. Those demands are also part of American culture, to the extent that boomers have multiple and ongoing midlife crises. The self's need to adapt to the demands of the self is perhaps the strongest reason to reassess our lives in our forties, fifties, and sixties—years in which we also realize that our passions, usually unburied from the past, must be roused before it's too late.

When I could no longer ignore my individuating desire to write professionally, I quit, at fifty, my tenured job as a professor of English. Before I did, I worried that my decision was misguided. I asked friends what they thought; I assumed they'd say, "You shouldn't do it. What will you do for money? What will happen to your health care?" My fears were dead wrong. In fact, no one spoke *my* fears. Rather, they told me how much they envied my daring. In their minds, I was enacting as much my choice as I was my generation's impulse to drop out, a graying cultural touchstone, which we believe is there for the taking no matter how old we get.

RECENTLY I WAS LISTENING to Bob Dylan sing "Not Dark Yet" from the album *Time Out of Mind*. Something about Dylan's vocal struck me. It was not just his cryptic sarcasm or his trademark scoff, evident in his singing style since "Don't Think Twice, It's All Right." It was Dylan's presence in the room. That testimonial voice, much like James Baldwin had sounded to me from the page twenty years earlier, was actual and intoned, inescapably so. Dylan's singing carried the hard rain of its truth, a fact he underscored when, to Martin Scorsese, he explained his artistic purpose, albeit with an existential gloss: "I wrote the songs so I could sing them." His songs were written so *he* could sing them. They were *his,* unlike, say Mozart's arias, which were intended for performers. Though others have sung his work, Dylan's self-possession of his songs means that his performance is the way they sound best. It may be one reason why, since 1988, Dylan has been on the "Never Ending Tour." As the tour's unofficial Web site notes, Dylan's concertizing allows him "to reformulate and re-interpret his art through performance. Playing a song was not about recreating a record. A song would live again, changing into a new or mutated form on stage." Dylan is a peripatetic troubadour, one foot in the Provençal tradition, the other in the electronic age.

Such vocalizing has been the norm in American culture for more than four decades. Vocal artistry is, of course, individual. We think of bards like Dylan and Joni Mitchell, poets like Allen Ginsberg and Maya Angelou, comedians like Richard Pryor and George Carlin, satirists like Amy Sedaris and Stephen Colbert, singers like Andrea Bocelli and Mariah Carey, even bloviators like Rush Limbaugh and Christopher Hitchens—their *heard* voices and the familiarity they engender make them, which is to say their personalities, compelling. (*What* they are saying is another matter.) I think the out-loud electronic world has left the page-quiet literary work feeling jealous, perhaps inadequate. Not to be heard in this culture is a death sentence. Memoir's audible quality has arisen more as an equivalent, less as a challenge, to the ubiquity of records, audiobooks, movies, and TV; camcorders, mobiles, video phones, and iPods; radio commentary, poetry slams, and podcasts. For literature, memoir is carrying what is essential to advancing any art these days: the *buzz.*

Memoir's voice also carries a likeableness, in a way the cold irony of postmodern literature does not.[1] We *like* how Mikal Gilmore, Jill Ciment, Mitch Albom, Lucy Grealy sound as they share their stories. Such willingness to appeal to what's personal meets us where we live. Listen to the opening sentence of Natalie Kusz's *Road Song* (1990): "Our first months in Alaska, that one long summertime before I was hurt, were hard—in the way, I think, that all immigrants' lives must be hard—but they were also very grand, full of wood fires and campgrounds, full of people and the stories they told at night when we ate all together, full of clean dust that we washed from our bodies with water carried home from cold springs" (5). Notice Kusz's use of *we;* notice the *good* hardship, the *homeyness:* after she foreshadows her "hurt," we warm to the "wood fires" and "campgrounds"; the "stories told at night" during the "one long summertime"; the "clean dust," washed away with "water carried home from cold springs." The tenderness of home. The tale of the immigrant, a rite of passage for nearly every American. Who among us doesn't want to be confided to by this writer's voice? That the bad stuff is coming doesn't seem to matter as much once we know the family is self-reliant, perhaps as ours once was. (It goes without saying that the maudlin memoirists prey on this tune and abuse it with impunity.)

In another vein, who can resist David Sedaris—on tape, on David Letterman, at a book signing, on the pages of *Me Talk Pretty One Day* (2000)—and his voice's comic flatness, its circus-like musicality? Despite the affect, Sedaris is also everyday-sounding, recalling an eccentric family, stupid jobs, bumbling French in France after six weeks of lessons. How *us* that is! How unlike the disembodied, fantastic voices of much contemporary fiction, whose gritty or alien or omniscient or after-life narrators feel artificial, ghoulish, and mocking.

Memoir is the speaking "I" of a trusting author, walking hand in hand with the reader down a path both know well. It mirrors the open-faced trait of Americans and their speech. It remains open to the nostalgic and the sentimental. It personalizes horror. It belongs equally to a professional writer and a dockworker, a home health-care nurse and your Uncle Donny. Even President

George W. Bush works hard at making his voice sound off-the-cuff, unaffected, memoiristic, sincere. Indeed, he can sound fully believable. Who was the political philosopher that most influenced him? "Christ," he said, "because he changed my heart." Good line.

In a culture of media clips and "instant communication," the memoir takes its meditative time to discover and deliver its message. Amid the blab of ideologues and TV monologists, the memoir suffers few pretensions, academic fixations, Brahmin inflections, newspeak analysis. It possesses an authentic American voice, and the memoirist writes in it. Americans like being talked to in that voice. At times, at length. At times, it is the only thing that penetrates their loneliness and fear, especially in the age of terror.

Lying in Public

Still, pulling the curtain back on all this vocal verisimilitude, in memoir or any contemporary art, tells only part of the story. A dark wing remains. So much of what our culture expresses as personal is *not* intimate and meaningful—it's trite, unthought-out, venomous. Despite the emotion-friendly airwaves, personal revelation is everywhere and nowhere. What the out-loud culture showcases in breadth it lacks in depth. Sound bites and talking heads forbid the complicated, the psychological, the personally messy from going on too long. *In the thirty seconds we have left, could you give our viewers a sense of why you wrote your book?* Consider that in the confession booth of TV what unfolds is never the truth. It's bullshit. Public reckonings, demanded of Jimmy Swaggart, Bill Clinton, Dick Cheney, James Frey, and others for their moral transgressions, may sound frank, but, when scrutinized, the testament is rubbish. It matters little whether what one is fessing up to is true. The only real test is sincerity, which can be easily faked.

How much we are taken in—at least, in the moment—by the sonorously familiar. How many of us believed President Clinton when he said, "I did not have sex with that woman, Miss Lewinsky"? How many of us were convinced by President Bush's 2003 claim, "Mission accomplished"? We always want to believe more than we want to question. Memoir will not change that fact. Far worse, however, is our acceptance that what is uttered by those in positions of any power, then televised to the masses, cannot be the truth. It can only be spin, the story masquerading to save face, to stay clear of the so-called reality-based community and perpetuate the fantasy of control.

I would argue that memoir is taking the lead, among other dissenting voices, against any form of media misrepresentation be it the staged public confession, the press release, public relations, carefully worded statements of denial or apology. Writers and some commentators are telling us to distrust what's telegenically spoken, to recognize that its ring of "truthiness" and other tricks of the authoritarian dissembler are a kind of devil's bargain. Perhaps memoir's genius is this: to use its intimate-sounding voice, so culturally recognizable already, to cast doubt on the easy believability of that voice. In the memoir itself, this tension is embodied by a willingness to speak of difficult matters and a willingness to question what's being spoken. Also, because of the form's ease with narrative, its likeable self-regard, it's quite good at getting our attention, after which it's able to steer our attentiveness where it wants. In *Leaving Church: A Memoir of Faith* (2006), Barbara Brown Taylor says that first I'm going to guide you into a story about finding faith, where you'll feel and understand what led me to become an Episcopal priest and remain one for twenty years. But then I'm going to guide you just as carefully into what led me to lose that faith. Can anyone imagine explaining such a long-term fall from certainty in fifteen minutes, under lights and camera, even to Bill Moyers? Our supposition is that we present ourselves to others, especially in public forums, only when we know ahead of time what we're going to say: think political punditry, think sales seminar, think doctor talk, think talking points. Memoir is reminding us that its largely essayistic direction allows readers and writers not to know ahead of time what will be said. And to preserve that not-knowing, that tentativeness, is vital to the memoir's story.

A Culture of Selves

I want to end by returning to the idea that the memoir may be developing a relational link between culture and self. One of the things we've learned, at least those of us who endured the conformist zeal of 1950s America—the world our communist-fearing fathers and mothers inculcated in us—is that we don't trust the terror-mongering that cultures create, whether it's selling bomb shelters or electing extremist politicians. Many of us don't trust the revived terror-mongering culture we are living in since 9/11. Is there some sort of attack on this fear-based culture, a kind of social critique from the personal perspective, that the memoir might offer now? Could memoir, while it deconstructs the individual's self-deception, also be exposing our culture's self-delusion? I think that unlocking the self-deception of an individual is a counterpart or an equivalent to unlocking the self-deception of a culture, insofar as a culture can possess a self-identity. This may be what the memoir is awakening to as its social purpose—to bring personal testimony to a society imbued with media brainwashing and ideological imprisonment so as to subvert or depose that authority.

In 1997, Mary Karr responded in an interview with Salon.com that "people want some sort of moral compass, and the subjective"—evident in the memoir form—"suddenly has power it hasn't had before because all of the measures of how we are doing—the church, community life, religious or government leaders, certain kinds of values, family—no longer mean what they once did." That the personal would be key in bringing back our "moral compass" is fascinating. What's fallen from our lives—at least, from the lives of those who have left the patriarchal behind—is our parents' rectitude, its belief in an authoritarian center. In its place is personal inquiry, individual knowing, moral relativism. This is not a new endeavor; there's a long tradition of using literary forms to press social inquiry. Memoir is judging the paradoxes of public and private truth-telling in our time much as the essay inquired into the claims of science and philosophy during the Enlightenment, the novel critiqued the expanding bourgeois class in Europe in the early nineteenth century, and the slave narrative demonstrated the ghastliness of African bondage before the Civil War.

Enlightened thinking by way of personal experience is taking many breathless forms these days, and not just in the memoir. I have been moved by Sam Harris's *The End of Faith: Religion, Terror, and the Future of Reason* (2005), a polemical book Harris wrote following a long apprenticeship during which he personally explored Eastern and Western religious traditions. Harris is most critical of Western religions and the liberal notion of religious tolerance. He reflects on the power of free thought in a world that remains enthralled to religious belief, assailing theocratic societies all over the globe that are unwilling to change. "If religion addresses a genuine sphere of understanding and human necessity," he writes, "then it should be susceptible to *progress;* its doctrines should become more useful, rather than less. Progress in religion, as in other fields, would have to be a matter of *present* inquiry, not the mere reiteration of past doctrine. Whatever is true now should be *discoverable* now, and describable in terms that are not an outright affront to the rest of what we know about the world" (22).

How commonsensical it is to place present inquiry above past doctrine; it may be the only way civilization will survive. Progress is germane to the scientist and, I would argue, to the artist as well. Memoir writers believe like Harris and other rational thinkers that there are new means by which we can understand why we have—why we've always had—such a predilection to believe our self-deceptions. The science of mind (neuroscience) and the study of consciousness (psychology) can ground us in this pursuit. Our culture may be moving toward a truth-telling mode like memoir, which questions traditions of myth-based literature, in the same way that our society may be moving toward science, which counters traditions of myth-based belief. Science and art are more than coproductive ways of exploring truth and deceit. Science and art are complementary. *How* we convince ourselves of what is real, individually and culturally, can be studied by scientists as fully as it can be engaged by artists. To waken from superstition—be it religious or literary, cultural or personal—is the goal of human inquiry as well as the memoir's reason for being.

Notes

Chapter One

1. The short memoir or personal essay is everywhere. At *Newsweek,* the weekly column My Turn is a personal narrative: the magazine receives fifteen hundred unsolicited pieces every week. At the *New Yorker* the short memoir is labeled Personal History. Most daily newspapers or their Sunday sections publish personal writing: for example, the *San Francisco Chronicle's* Sunday Magazine includes My Word, a 900-word back-page memoir piece. Personal essays are found at the *New York Times:* in the Sunday Style section called Modern Love and in the *New York Times Magazine* called Lives. Alice Sebold's *Lucky* began as a personal narrative in the *New York Times Magazine:* an editor read it and insisted she write the book, a not uncommon way in which full-length memoir is initiated. I have written of the testimonial works of James Baldwin: they are now in *James Baldwin: Collected Essays,* 1998. Among the best memoiristic essay collections I know are those by Meghan Daum, *My Misspent Youth* (2001); Leonard Kriegel, *Flying Solo: Reimagining Manhood, Courage, and Loss* (1998); Phillip Lopate, *Portrait of My Body* (1996); and Annie Dillard, *Teaching a Stone to Talk: Expeditions and Encounters* (1982). The following short memoir anthologies are essential: *The Beholder's Eye: A Collection of America's Finest Personal Journalism,* edited by Walt Harrington (2005); *In Brief: Short Takes on the Personal,* edited by Judith Kitchen and Mary Paumier Jones (1999); *The Norton Book of American Autobiography,*

edited by Jay Parini (1999); *The Art of the Personal Essay,* edited by Phillip Lopate (1994); *California Childhood: Recollections and Stories of the Golden State,* edited by Gary Soto (1988); and *The Best American Essays,* an annual. Some of the finer literary journals that publish personal essays and short memoir (under six thousand words) are the *Sun, Fourth Genre,* the *Missouri Review, Witness,* and the *North American Review.*

2. Anne Frank began her diary on her thirteenth birthday, June 12, 1942, and stopped two years later on August 1, 1944, when she and her family were removed from the annex and freight-trained to Auschwitz. The *Diary* has been published (by Anne's father and others) in a series of severely edited editions, beginning in 1947. My article "'In Spite of Everything': The Definitive Indefinite Anne Frank," *Antioch Review* 58, no. 1 (Winter 2000): 40–54, describes why Anne's revelations were censored and what the book says now after those revelations were restored.

3. Here's a list of good books that analyze the memoir universe: by era (memoir is the trend, autobiography, the tradition); by technique (narration, characterization, description, plot); by subject (illness, loss, family, romance, person, place, event, feminist, and so on); by traditional form (letter, diary, journal, travel essay, reflective essay, personal narrative, memoir). Vivian Gornick's *The Situation and the Story* (2000) is a brilliant essay about short and long memoir forms; she is a superb close reader of memoir style. Jill Ker Conway's *When Memory Speaks: Reflections on Autobiography* (1998) takes the reader from St. Augustine and Rousseau to Jan Morris and Bruce McCall. Surveying how autobiography is shaped by culture, Conway is insightful on the "agency" difference between men and women: memoirs by men feature their built-in agency while memoirs by women depict women acquiring agency. Nancy K. Miller's *Getting Personal: Feminist Occasions and Other Autobiographical Acts* (1991) showcases she who first dared to merge literary criticism, women's studies, and personal narrative. Philippe

Lejeune's difficult but rewarding *On Autobiography* (1989) applies the structuralist's spade to mostly French autobiographers. William Zinsser's *Inventing the Truth: The Art and Craft of Memoir* (1987) includes essays about craft and impetus by memoirists, biographers, and a few autobiographical novelists. Robert Lyons's *Autobiography: A Reader for Writers* (1984) is the finest set of analytical introductions to the traditional autobiographical forms ever written. Lyons is the most astute thinker about the formal elements of autobiography I've read; it's a literary crime that his anthology remains out of print. Roy Pascal's *Design and Truth in Autobiography* (1960) takes apart traditional autobiography and emphasizes that in writing their story writers "struggle with the truth," the struggle being the point, not the arrival at the truth. Other joys include Maureen Murdock, *Unreliable Truth: On Memory and Memoir* (2003); *Encyclopedia of Life Writing: Biographical and Autobiographical Forms*, edited by Margaretta Jolly (2001); *The Business of Memory*, edited by Charles Baxter (1999); Patricia Hampl, *I Could Tell You Stories: Sojourns in the Land of Memory* (1999); as well as articles or books on memoir and autobiography by Rockwell Gray, Barrett J. Mandel, Paul John Eakin, Albert E. Stone, Timothy Dow Adams, James M. Cox, James Olney, and Lee Gutkind, a male club, to be sure.

Chapter Two

1. One of the more fascinating elements of the James Frey controversy in 2006 over his *A Million Little Pieces* (2003) is that Frey believed the culture and other memoir writers were telling him that the facts in memoir have wiggle room: 5 percent fictionalization (exaggeration or lying), he said, is okay for memoirists because the form "allows" it. Where this number came from is itself a myth. My later chapters on how writers build trust in the memoir will address this penchant for claiming to know what's true, especially by

those who are lifelong manipulators—addicts and confabulators as well as those with impaired memories and severe depression. It's important to note here that even the smallest percentage of a falsified factual truth (Frey's claim that he was in jail eighty-seven days instead of three hours) ruined whatever emotional truth he may have conveyed as well as called into question every factual truth in the book. If his lies are that bold in one part of the story, what's to keep him from lying in other parts?

Chapter Eleven

1. Persona and artist are endlessly construed. Here's a publisher blurb for *Writing Dylan: The Songs of a Lonesome Traveler,* by Larry David Smith (2005), which may or may not be what the book's about. "Whether he wanted to or not, Bob Dylan spoke for a generation. In this bold and comprehensive study, Larry David Smith makes the case that 'Bob Dylan' is a persona carefully crafted by the former Robert Zimmerman of Hibbing, Minnesota. Granted unprecedented use of Dylan's lyrics, Smith analyzes the poet's narratives, characters, plots, and values to reveal his mission-oriented approach to art." I find it absurd that the self-protective Dylan gave Smith "unprecedented use" of anything.

Chapter Thirteen

1. If James Frey taught us anything, it is that not only can emotional truth deceive the reader, who may not care whether a given incident is made up (Oprah Winfrey's original statement: "We support the book because we recognize that there have been thousands and hundreds of thousands of people whose lives have been changed by this book"), but the impact of one's emotional truth is lost if the author is shown to have altered core details (one of Oprah's comebacks: "No, the *lie* of it. That's a lie. It's not an idea, James. That's

a lie"). But rewind the tape before his claims were investigated. The "truth" he achieved was the province of narrative; though root canals without Novocaine make one cringe, the ex–drug addict convinced us via storytelling that he handled the experience. His sole reliance on narrative to present a heroic self (the mental disorder is called delusions of grandeur or grandiosity) should have tipped us off that his story was way over the top. In the end, he admitted to being not "as introspective as I should have been." For some fiction-based reason, Frey thought that he had to narrate everything; he never got to learn for himself *in the memoir* how he knew what he knew.

Chapter Fourteen

I, Bentley's is an example of what I would call the memoir of passion. Hers is sophomoric in its self-absorption, which should be obvious. To dump the lot by cursing pulp versions of the form, however, is meaningless. Memoir-reviewer Jeff Gundy comments, "Surely we will not stamp out bad writing—of which there will always be plenty, of every sort—by opposing whole genres on the grounds that they include some" (774). There are several writers who interrogate and celebrate their passions more dispassionately. Some passions are intellectual, others are physical; both cultivate something outside the self, which returns some opposition. In Janet Malcolm's *Reading Chekhov: A Critical Journey* (2001), she goes on a literary pilgrimage in search of his ghost in St. Petersburg, Moscow, and Yalta, meditating on his life, his work, and his death, from consumption, at forty-four. Malcolm is distrustful of literary fame as well as her own prying interests. While enduring pushy Russian tour guides, she uncovers enigmas in the culture's honoring of its most beloved author. Other writers gifted with this personal-critical approach (often of literary figures or art objects) are Geoff Dyer, Craig Seligman, and Michael Kimmelman.

Chapter Fifteen

1. One irony is that very little of the vocal identity of memoirists (except the loquacious Frank McCourt and his brother, Malachy, who appeared regularly in the mid-1990s on C-Span and Book TV) comes from their out-loud reading voices. Having said that, however, I note the growth of the audible author—book reading, book festival, book-on-tape, book tour. The swampy drawl of Rick Bragg's voice embodies his story better than any actor can. In fact, most memoirists surpass the trained affability of the Broadway actor once the writer is recorded, sounding and owning his actual words in his actual voice.

Memoirs

This list is meant to reveal the variety and the originality of the form. Memoirs discussed in the text, whether at length or briefly, are noted with an *.

Before 1987: Important Precursors

1. Anaïs Nin. *The Diary of Anaïs Nin.* 1931–74. Edited by Gunther Stuhlmann. 7 vols. New York: Harcourt Brace Jovanovich, 1966–80.

2. George Orwell. *Down and Out in Paris and London.* New York: Harper & Brothers, 1933.

3. Henry Miller. *Tropic of Cancer.* Paris: Obelisk Press, 1934; New York: Grove Press, 1961.

4. *F. Scott Fitzgerald. *The Crack-Up.* 1936. New York: New Directions, 1956.

5. *Virginia Woolf. "A Sketch." 1939/40. In *Moments of Being.* 2nd ed. New York: Harcourt Brace Jovanovich, 1985.

6. *Anne Frank. *The Diary of a Young Girl.* 1942–44. First published (in Dutch) 1947. First American edition 1952. New York: Doubleday, 1995.

7. Richard Wright. *Black Boy.* New York: Harper & Brothers, 1945.

8. Primo Levi. *Survival in Auschwitz.* 1947. New York: Simon & Schuster, 1996.

9. *John Gunther. *Death Be Not Proud: A Memoir.* New York: Harper & Row, 1949.

10.   *Alfred Kazin. *A Walker in the City.* New York: Harcourt, Brace, 1951.

11.   *Mary McCarthy. *Memories of a Catholic Girlhood.* New York: Harcourt, Brace,, 1957.

12.   Elie Wiesel. *Night.* 1958. New York: Hill & Wang, 1960.

13.   Carl Jung. *Memories, Dreams, Reflections.* New York: Random House, 1963.

14.   Frank Conroy. *Stop-Time.* New York: Viking, 1967.

15.   Willie Morris. *North Toward Home.* Boston: Houghton Mifflin, 1967.

16.   Anne Moody. *Coming of Age in Mississippi.* New York: Dell, 1968.

17.   J. R. Ackerley. *My Father and Myself.* New York: Coward-McCann, 1969.

18.   *Maya Angelou. *I Know Why the Caged Bird Sings.* New York: Random House, 1970.

19.   *Maxine Hong Kingston. *The Woman Warrior: Memoirs of a Girlhood among Ghosts.* New York: Alfred A. Knopf, 1976.

20.   Geoffrey Wolff. *The Duke of Deception: Memories of My Father.* New York: Random House, 1979.

21.   Wright Morris. *Will's Boy: A Memoir.* New York: Harper & Row, 1981.

22.   Susan Allen Toth. *Blooming: A Small-Town Girlhood.* Boston: Little, Brown, 1981.

23.   Russell Baker. *Growing Up.* New York: Congdon & Weed, 1982.

24.   James McConkey. *Court of Memory.* New York: E. P. Dutton, 1983.

25.   Eudora Welty. *One Writer's Beginnings.* Cambridge, MA: Harvard University Press, 1984.

After 1987

26.   *Sylvia Fraser. *My Father's House.* New York: Ticknor & Fields, 1987.

27. *Vivian Gornick. *Fierce Attachments: A Memoir.* New York: Simon & Schuster, 1987.

28. *Annie Dillard. *An American Childhood.* New York: Harper & Row, 1987.

29. Annie Ernaux. *A Woman's Story.* 1988. Translated by Tanya Leslie. New York: Four Walls Eight Windows, 1991.

30. *Tobias Wolff. *This Boy's Life: A Memoir.* New York: Atlantic Monthly Press, 1988.

31. *Jill Ker Conway. *The Road from Coorain.* New York: Alfred A. Knopf, 1989.

32. John Updike. *Self-Consciousness: Memoirs.* New York: Alfred A. Knopf, 1989.

33. Reynolds Price. *Clear Pictures: First Loves, First Guides.* New York: Atheneum, 1989.

34. *Richard Rhodes. *A Hole in the World: An American Boyhood.* New York: Simon & Schuster, 1990.

35. *William Styron. *Darkness Visible: A Memoir of Madness.* New York: Random House, 1990.

36. *Natalie Kusz. *Road Song: A Memoir.* New York: Harper-Collins, 1990.

37. *Bernard Cooper. *Maps to Anywhere.* Athens: University of Georgia Press, 1990.

38. Andrew H. Malcolm. *Someday: The Story of a Mother and Her Son.* New York: Alfred A. Knopf, 1991.

39. Elizabeth Swados. *The Four of Us: A Family Memoir.* New York: Farrar, Straus & Giroux, 1991.

40. *Deborah Digges, *Fugitive Spring: Coming of Age in the '50s and '60s.* New York: Alfred A. Knopf, 1991.

41. Phillip Roth. *Patrimony: A True Story.* New York: Simon & Schuster, 1991.

42. *Annie Ernaux. *Simple Passion.* 1991. Translated by Tanya Leslie. New York: Ballantine, 1993.

43. Richard Selzer. *Down from Troy: A Doctor Comes of Age.* New York: William Morrow, 1992.

44. Paul Monette. *Becoming a Man: Half a Life Story*. New York: Harcourt Brace Jovanovich, 1992.

45. *Anatole Broyard. *Intoxicated by My Illness*. New York: Clarkson Potter, 1992.

46. *Beverly Lowry. *Crossed Over: A Murder, A Memoir*. New York: Alfred A. Knopf, 1992.

47. Christopher Hudson. *Spring Street Summer: The Search for a Lost Paradise*. New York: Alfred A. Knopf, 1993.

48. Chris Orfutt. *The Same River Twice: A Memoir*. New York: Simon & Schuster, 1993.

49. *William Loizeaux. *Anna: A Daughter's Life*. New York: Arcade, 1993.

50. Blake Morrison. *And When Did You Last See Your Father?* London: Granta, 1993.

51. *Susanna Kaysen. *Girl, Interrupted*. New York: Random House, 1993.

52. Richard Selzer. *Raising the Dead: A Doctor's Encounter with His Own Mortality*. New York: Viking Penguin, 1993.

53. Brent Staples. *Parallel Time: Growing Up in Black and White*. New York: Random House, 1994.

54. Erica Jong. *Fear of Fifty*. New York: Random House, 1994.

55. Lionel Dahmer. *A Father's Story*. New York: William Morrow, 1994.

56. *Elizabeth Wurtzel. *Prozac Nation: Young and Depressed in America*. Boston: Houghton Mifflin, 1994.

57. Dennis Covington. *Salvation on Sand Mountain: Snake Handling and Redemption in Southern Appalachia*. New York: Addison-Wesley, 1994.

58. *Lucy Grealy. *Autobiography of a Face*. Boston: Houghton Mifflin, 1994.

59. Mikal Gilmore. *Shot in the Heart*. New York: Doubleday, 1994.

60. Robb Forman Dew. *The Family Heart: A Memoir of When Our Son Came Out*. New York: Addison-Wesley, 1994.

61. John Edgar Wideman. *Fatheralong: A Meditation on Fathers and Sons, Race and Society.* New York: Random House, 1994.

62. Carolyn See. *Dreaming: Hard Luck and Good Times in America.* Berkeley: University of California Press, 1995.

63. William H. Pritchard. *English Papers: A Teaching Life.* Saint Paul: Graywolf Press, 1995.

64. *Kay Redfield Jamison. *An Unquiet Mind: A Memoir of Moods and Madness.* New York: Alfred A. Knopf, 1995.

65. *Richard Hoffman. *Half the House: A Memoir.* New York: Harcourt Brace, 1995.

66. *Mary Karr. *The Liars' Club.* New York: Viking Penguin, 1995.

67. *Mark Salzman. *Lost in Place.* New York: Random House, 1995.

68. *Frank McCourt. *Angela's Ashes.* New York: Scribner, 1996.

69. Lynne Sharon Schwartz. *Ruined by Reading: A Life in Books.* Boston: Beacon Press, 1996

70. Caroline Knapp. *Drinking: A Love Story.* New York: The Dial Press, 1996.

71. *Harold Brodkey. *This Wild Darkness: The Story of My Death.* New York: Henry Holt, 1996.

72. *Nuala O'Faolain, *Are You Somebody? The Accidental Memoir of a Dublin Woman.* Dublin: New Island, 1996.

73. James Carroll. *An American Requiem: God, My Father, and the War That Came Between Us.* Boston: Houghton Mifflin, 1996.

74. Jill Ciment. *Half a Life: A Memoir.* New York: Crown, 1996.

75. Hilton Als. *The Women.* New York: Farrar, Straus & Giroux, 1996.

76. *James McBride. *The Color of Water: A Black Man's Tribute to His White Mother.* New York: Riverhead, 1996.

77. Anne Schreiber. *Light Years.* New York: Lyons & Buford, 1996.

78. Bernard Cooper. *Truth Serum: Memoirs.* Boston: Houghton Mifflin, 1996.

79. Pang-Mei Natasha Chang. *Bound Feet and Western Dress.* New York: Doubleday, 1996.

80. Calvin Trillin. *Messages from My Father.* New York: Farrar, Straus & Giroux, 1996.

81. *Rick Bragg. *All Over but the Shoutin'.* New York: Random House, 1997.

82. *Kathryn Harrison. *The Kiss: A Memoir.* New York: Random House, 1997.

83. *Geoff Dyer. *Out of Sheer Rage: Wrestling with D. H. Lawrence.* London: Little Brown, 1997.

84. Phyllis Rose. *The Year of Reading Proust: A Memoir in Real Time.* New York: Scribner, 1997.

85. *Mitch Albom. *Tuesdays with Morrie: An Old Man, A Young Man, and Life's Greatest Lesson.* New York: Doubleday, 1997.

86. Linda Katherine Cutting. *Memory Slips: A Memoir of Music and Healing.* New York: HarperCollins, 1997.

87. *Lauren Slater. *Prozac Diary.* New York: Random House, 1998.

88. *Molly Peacock. *Paradise: Piece by Piece.* New York: Riverhead, 1998.

89. *Catherine Texier. *Breakup: The End of a Love Story.* New York: Doubleday, 1998.

90. *Mark Doty. *Firebird: A Memoir.* New York: HarperCollins, 1999.

91. *Alice Sebold. *Lucky.* New York: Scribner, 1999.

92. Mary von Schrader Jarrell. *Remembering Randall: A Memoir of Poet, Critic, and Teacher Randall Jarrell.* New York: HarperCollins, 1999.

93. *Annie Dillard. *For the Time Being.* New York: Alfred A. Knopf, 1999.

94. *David Sedaris. *Me Talk Pretty One Day.* Boston: Little Brown, 2000.

95. Elizabeth Fox Gordon. *The Mockingbird Years.* New York: Basic Books, 2000.

96. *Dave Eggers. *A Heartbreaking Work of Staggering Genius.* New York: Random House, 2000.

97. Mary Karr. *Cherry.* New York: Viking Penguin, 2000.

98. Larry Woiwode. *What I Think I Did: A Season of Survival in Two Acts.* New York: Basic Books, 2000.

99. *Lauren Slater. *Lying: A Metaphorical Memoir.* New York: Random House, 2000.

100. *Mark Doty. *Still Life with Oysters and Lemon.* Boston: Beacon Press, 2001.

101. *Janet Malcolm. *Reading Chekhov.* New York: Random House, 2001.

102. Augusten Burroughs. *Running with Scissors: A Memoir.* New York: St. Martin's Press, 2002.

103. Alec Wilkinson. *My Mentor: A Young Man's Friendship with William Maxwell.* Boston: Houghton Mifflin, 2002.

104. *Azar Nafisi. *Reading Lolita in Tehran: A Memoir in Books.* New York: Random House, 2003.

105. *Anthony Swofford. *Jarhead: A Marine's Chronicle of the Gulf War and Other Battles.* New York: Scribner, 2003.

106. Floyd Skloot. *In the Shadow of Memory.* Lincoln: University of Nebraska Press, 2003.

107. David Denby. *American Sucker.* Boston: Little Brown, 2004.

108. *Laurie Alberts. *Fault Line.* Lincoln: University of Nebraska Press, 2004.

109. Craig Seligman. *Sontag and Kael: Opposites Attract Me.* New York: Counterpoint, 2004.

110. *Kathryn Harrison. *The Mother Knot: A Memoir.* New York: Random House, 2004.

111. Joan Didion. *Where I Was From.* New York: Alfred A. Knopf, 2004.

112. Bob Dylan. *Chronicles: Volume One.* New York: Simon & Schuster, 2004.

113.   *Toni Bentley. *The Surrender: An Erotic Memoir.* New York: HarperCollins, 2004.

114.   *Joseph Lelyveld. *Omaha Blues: A Memory Loop.* New York: Farrar, Straus & Giroux, 2005.

115.   *Judith Moore. *Fat Girl: A True Story.* New York: Hudson Street Press, 2005.

116.   *James Atlas. *My Life in the Middle Ages: A Survivor's Tale.* New York: HarperCollins, 2005.

117.   *Jeanette Walls. *The Glass Castle: A Memoir.* New York: Scribner, 2005.

118.   Sean Wilsey. *Oh the Glory of It All.* New York: Penguin Press, 2005.

119.   *Joan Didion. *The Year of Magical Thinking.* New York: Alfred A. Knopf, 2005.

120.   *Barbara Brown Taylor. *Leaving Church: A Memoir of Faith.* San Francisco: Harper, 2006.

121.   Bill Buford. *Heat: An Amateur's Adventures as Kitchen Slave, Line Cook, Pasta-Maker, and Apprentice to a Dante-Quoting Butcher in Tuscany.* New York: Alfred A. Knopf, 2006.

122.   Terri Jentz. *Strange Piece of Paradise: A Return to the American West to Investigate My Attempted Murder—and Solve the Riddle of Myself.* New York: Farrar, Straus & Giroux, 2006.

123.   Ken Dornstein. *The Boy Who Fell out of the Sky: A True Story.* New York: Random House, 2006.

124.   Donald Antrim. *The Afterlife.* New York: Farrar, Straus & Giroux, 2006.

125.   Bernard Cooper. *The Bill from My Father.* New York: Simon & Schuster, 2006.

Works Cited

Auerbach, Erich. *Mimesis: The Representation of Reality in Western Literature*. Translated by Willard R. Trask. Princeton: Princeton University Press, 1953.

Baker, Russell. "Fathers and Son." Review of *Omaha Blues: A Memory Loop*, by Joseph Lelyveld. *New York Review of Books*, 26 April 2005, 16–18.

Baldwin, James. *Collected Essays*. New York: Library of America, 1998.

Bentley, Toni. *The Surrender: An Erotic Memoir*. New York: Harper-Collins, 2004.

Bly, Robert. *A Little Book on the Human Shadow*. Edited by William Booth. New York: HarperCollins, 1988.

"Bob Dylan and the Never Ending Tour Band," http://www.members .tripod.com/mathematicalmusic/neverending/neverending.html.

Bragg, Rick. *All Over but the Shoutin'*. New York: Random House, 1997.

Cather, Willa. *Stories, Poems, and Other Writings*. New York: Library of America, 1992.

Cooper, Bernard. *Maps to Anywhere*. Athens: University of Georgia Press, 1990.

Digges, Deborah. *Fugitive Spring: Coming of Age in the '50s and '60s*. New York: Alfred A. Knopf, 1991.

Dillard, Annie. *For the Time Being*. New York: Alfred A. Knopf, 1999.

Doctorow, E. L. Introduction to Fitzgerald, *The Jazz Age*.

Doty, Mark. *Firebird: A Memoir.* New York: HarperCollins, 1999.

Duras, Marguerite. *Practicalities: Marguerite Duras Speaks to Jerome Beaujour.* Translated by Barbara Bray. New York: Grove Weidenfeld, 1990.

Eggers, Dave. *A Heartbreaking Work of Staggering Genius.* New York: Random House, 2000.

Engel, Susan. *Context Is Everything: The Nature of Memory.* New York: W. H. Freeman, 1999.

Ernaux, Annie. *Simple Passion.* New York: Seven Stories Press, 2003.

Fitzgerald, F. Scott. "The Crack-Up." In *The Jazz Age.* New York: New Directions Bibelot, 1996.

Fraser, Sylvia. *My Father's House: A Memoir of Incest and Healing.* New York: Ticknor and Fields, 1987.

Frye, Northrop. *Anatomy of Criticism: Four Essays.* Princeton, NJ: Princeton University Press, 1957.

Gornick, Vivian. "A Memoirist Defends Her Words." *Salon* (8 August 2003), http://dir.salon.com/story/books/feature/2003/08/12/memoir_writing/index_np.html.

———. *The Situation and the Story: The Art of Personal Narrative.* New York: Farrar, Straus & Giroux, 2001.

Grealy, Lucy. *Autobiography of a Face.* Boston: Houghton Mifflin, 1994.

Gundy, Jeff. "Lives Worth Reading." *Georgia Review* 52, no. 4 (Winter 1998): 773–86.

Harris, Sam. *The End of Faith: Religion, Terror, and the Future of Reason.* New York: W. W. Norton, 2004.

Harrison, Kathryn. *The Mother Knot: A Memoir.* New York: Random House, 2004.

Heller, Zoe. "No Incest, and Only a Little Drink." *New York Times.* 15 March 1998, Sec 7, 10.

Higdon, David Leon. *Time and English Fiction.* London: Macmillan, 1977.

Hudgins, Andrew. "The Glass Anvil: Reflections on an Autobiography." In *The Glass Anvil*. Ann Arbor: University of Michigan Press, 1997. Originally published as "An Autobiographer's Lies," *American Scholar* 65 (1996): 541–53

Hulbert, Ann. "A Kiss Is Just a Kiss." Review of *The Kiss*, by Kathryn Harrison. *Slate* (19 March 1997), http://www.slate.com/id/2969.

Jefferson, Margo. "Facing truth about incest, in memoir and novel." *New York Times*, 29 May 1997, C13.

Jong, Erica. *Seducing the Demon: Writing for My Life*. New York: Tarcher, 2006.

Jung, C. J. *The Essential Jung*. Edited by Anthony Storr. New York: MJF, 1983.

Karr, Mary. "The Family Sideshow." Reading Group Guides.com, http://www.readinggroupguides.com/guides/liars_club.asp.

———. Interview by Dwight Garner. *Salon* (21 May 1997), http://www.salon.com/may97/karr970521.html.

———. *The Liars' Club: A Memoir*. New York: Viking Penguin, 1995.

Keefe, R. J. Review of *A Heartbreaking Work of Staggering Genius*, by Dave Eggers. Portico, http://www.portifex.com/Reading-Matter/Archive/HeartbreakingWork.htm.

Kotre, John. *White Gloves: How We Create Ourselves Through Memory*. New York: W. W. Norton, 1996.

Kriegel, Leonard. "From the Burning Bush the Autobiographical 'I.'" *Sewanee Review* 97 (Spring 1989): 202–19.

Kusz, Natalie. *Road Song: A Memoir*. New York: HarperCollins, 1990.

Lelyveld, Joseph. *Omaha Blues: A Memory Loop*. New York: Farrar, Straus & Giroux, 2005.

Lopate, Phillip, ed. *The Art of the Personal Essay: An Anthology from the Classical Era to the Present*. New York: Doubleday, 1994.

Lowry, Beverly. *Crossed Over: A Murder, a Memoir*. New York: Warner, 1992.

Lyall, Sarah. "A Wry Survivor of a World That Fell Apart." *New York Times,* 10 February 2000, E1.

Mandel, Barrett J. "The Past in Autobiography." *Soundings: An Interdisciplinary Journal* 64 (Spring 1981): 75–92.

McBride, James. *The Color of Water: A Black Man's Tribute to His White Mother.* New York: Riverhead, 1996.

McCarthy, Mary. *Memories of a Catholic Girlhood.* New York: Harcourt Brace Jovanovich, 1957.

McCourt, Frank. *Angela's Ashes: A Memoir.* New York: Scribner, 1996.

Mehegan, David. "Age Advances on a Literary Baby Boomer." *International Herald Tribune.* 26 April 2005, 10.

Moore, Judith. *Fat Girl: A True Story.* New York: Hudson Street Press, 2005.

Nafisi, Azar. *Reading Lolita in Tehran: A Memoir in Books.* New York: Random House, 2003.

O'Faolain, Nuala. *Are You Somebody? The Accidental Memoir of a Dublin Woman.* Dublin: New Island, 1996.

Pagels, Elaine. *Beyond Belief: The Secret Gospel of Thomas.* New York: Random House, 2003.

Parini, Jay, ed. *The Norton Book of American Autobiography.* New York: W. W. Norton, 1999.

Peacock, Molly. *Paradise, Piece by Piece.* New York: Riverhead, 1998.

Rumi. *The Soul of Rumi: A New Collection of Ecstatic Poems.* Translated by Coleman Barks. New York: HarperCollins, 2001.

Schiff, Stacy. "Never Trust a Memoirist." *American Scholar* 70 (Spring 2001): 63–69.

Sebold, Alice. Interview with Dave Weich. Powells.com, http://www .powells.com/authors/sebold.html.

Slater, Lauren. *Lying: A Metaphorical Memoir.* New York: Random House, 2000.

Sterling, Terry Greene. "Confessions of a Memoirist." *Salon* (1 August 2003), http://www.salon.com/books/feature/archives/2003/08/01/gornick/print.html.

Stevens, Anthony. *On Jung.* New York: Penguin, 1990.

Tuller, David. "Poet in the Making." Review of *Firebird: A Memoir,* by Mark Doty. *Washington Post* Book World, 16 January 2000, X09.

Wolff, Geoffrey. Introduction to *The Best American Essays 1989,* edited by Geoffrey Wolff. New York: Ticknor & Fields, 1989.

Woolf, Virginia. "A Sketch of the Past." In *Moments of Being,* edited by Jeanne Schulkind. 2nd ed. San Diego: Harcourt Brace Jovanovich, 1985.

Wurtzel, Elizabeth. *Prozac Nation: Young and Depressed in America.* Boston: Houghton Mifflin, 1994.

Zinsser, William K. *Inventing the Truth: The Art and Craft of Memoir.* Rev. ed. Boston: Houghton Mifflin, 1998.